# Quick Takes
# Rituals & Retreats

Robert W. Piercy
Jean E. Bross
Dirk deVries

©1999 Robert W. Piercy, Jean E. Bross and Dirk deVries

All rights reserved. No part of this publication may be reproduced in any form or by any means, electronic or mechanical, including photocopy, recording or any information storage and retrieval system, without permission in writing from the publisher, or unless otherwise specified.

Permission is hereby granted to reproduce and distribute the journal sheets, evaluation form and dramatic reading printed at the back of the book, pages 101-116.

The music suggested in the rituals comes from the publishers listed below. Contact them for further information.

Oregon Catholic Press (OCP)
5536 NE Hassalo
Portland, OR 97213
1-800-LITURGY (548-8749) or 503/281-1191
http://www.liturgy.com

GIA Publications, Inc.
7404 South Mason Avenue
Chicago, IL 60638
(800) GIA-1358 (442-1358) or (708) 496-3800
Fax: (708) 496-3828
http://www.giamusic.com
E-mail: custserv@giamusic.com


Living the Good News
   a division of The Morehouse Group
*Editorial Offices*
600 Grant Street, Suite 400
Denver, CO 80203
1-800-824-1813

James R. Creasey, Publisher

Dirk deVries, Editor

Jim Lemons, Layout

Val Price, Cover Design


Printed in the United States of America.

ISBN 1-889108-48-0

# TABLE OF CONTENTS

### Introduction: How to Use this Resource
Come On In! .................................................................................................................................................. 1
The Retreats ................................................................................................................................................... 1
    Starting the Process ................................................................................................................................ 1
    Recruit and Train Team Leaders ............................................................................................................. 1
    Maintaining the Team ............................................................................................................................. 2
    Witness Talks ........................................................................................................................................... 2
    Gather Supplies and Prepare the Environment ....................................................................................... 2
    Adapt, Adjust and Be Creative! .............................................................................................................. 2
    Pray .......................................................................................................................................................... 3
    Name Tags ............................................................................................................................................... 3
    Team Introductions .................................................................................................................................. 3
    Rules ........................................................................................................................................................ 3
    Overview of the Day ............................................................................................................................... 4
    Journal Reflections .................................................................................................................................. 4
    Evaluations .............................................................................................................................................. 4
    Departure ................................................................................................................................................ 4
The Rituals ..................................................................................................................................................... 4
    Linking Heart and Church ....................................................................................................................... 4
    Preparing for the Rituals ........................................................................................................................ 5
    Basic Premises of the Rituals ................................................................................................................. 5
    Using the Rituals with the Overnight Retreats ...................................................................................... 6

### Chapter 1: Family Issues Retreats
Retreat #1: Conflict in the Family—From Lose/Lose to Win/Win ............................................................. 8
    Ritual for Retreat #1: Making Peace .................................................................................................... 11
Retreat #2: Understanding Parents ............................................................................................................. 15
    Ritual for Retreat #2: Celebrating Our Roots ...................................................................................... 18
Retreat #3: Surviving Siblings .................................................................................................................... 21
    Ritual for Retreat #3: Celebrating the Gift of Brothers and Sisters ................................................... 24
Retreat #4: An Overnight Retreat on Family Issues .................................................................................. 26

### Chapter 2: Tough Emotions Retreats
Retreat #5: Stress and Depression .............................................................................................................. 32
    Ritual for Retreat #5: Comfort in Jesus' Presence ............................................................................... 34
Retreat #6: Anger and Hatred ..................................................................................................................... 37
    Ritual for Retreat #6: From Anger to Peace, From Hatred to Love .................................................... 40

Retreat #7: Facing Insecurity and Building Self-Esteem ............................................................................................................42
    Ritual for Retreat #7: Found by God ......................................................................................................................45
Retreat #8: An Overnight Retreat on Tough Emotions ..............................................................................................................47

## Chapter 3: World Problems Retreats
Retreat #9: Media Mania ........................................................................................................................................................53
    Ritual for Retreat #9: God's Peace in a Noisy World ............................................................................................56
Retreat #10: Globcl Concerns ................................................................................................................................................59
    Ritual for Retreat #10: From Hurting to Healing ....................................................................................................63
Retreat #11: Poverty and Wealth ............................................................................................................................................65
    Ritual for Retreat #11: Justice, Peace and Wholeness ..........................................................................................68
Retreat #12: An Overnight Retreat on World Problems............................................................................................................71

## Chapter 4: Relationship Issues Retreats
Retreat #13: Prejudice and Racism ........................................................................................................................................76
    Ritual for Retreat #13: Letting Go of Prejudice ......................................................................................................79
Retreat #14: Friendship Skills ..................................................................................................................................................82
    Ritual for Retreat #14: Friendship ..........................................................................................................................85
Retreat #15: Tough Choices ....................................................................................................................................................87
    Ritual for Retreat #15: From Darkness to Light......................................................................................................91
Retreat #16: An Overnight Retreat on Relationship Issues ......................................................................................................94

## Reproducible Handouts
Journal Sheets ......................................................................................................................................................................101
Evaluation Form ....................................................................................................................................................................114
The Prodigal Story (a dramatic reading) ..............................................................................................................................115

# INTRODUCTION

## HOW TO USE THIS RESOURCE

### COME ON IN!

Welcome to *Quick Takes Rituals and Retreats*. Combined with one or more volumes of *Quick Takes for Teens*, the volume you now hold enables you to create powerful retreat experiences for teens on a variety of contemporary topics.

We encourage you to read through this Introduction. In it we give you the background you need to conduct any of the retreats and rituals. (And note that the rituals can be used independently of the retreats!)

**To use this resource, you must own one or more of the four volumes of Quick Takes for Teens from Living the Good News**, because the majority of the activities used in the retreats are drawn from these books. Like the four books, each of which focuses on a broad topic of interest to teens, the retreats are likewise organized around these same themes:

- Retreats 1-4 correspond to *Quick Takes for Teens*, Volume 1: Family Issues.
- Retreats 5-8 correspond to *Quick Takes for Teens*, Volume 2: Tough Emotions.
- Retreats 9-12 correspond to *Quick Takes for Teens*, Volume 3: World Problems.
- Retreats 13-16 correspond to *Quick Takes for Teens*, Volume 4: Relationship Issues.

We produced *Quick Takes Rituals and Retreats* to meet the demand of youth leaders and catechists for ways to turn the "pick-and-choose" approach of *Quick Takes for Teens* into more structured sessions and retreats, supplemented with complementary rituals. If you need to order any of the volumes of *Quick Takes for Teens*, use the order form included at the back of the book, or you can call 1-800-824-1813 toll free.

### THE RETREATS

#### Starting the Process

Once you've decided to offer a retreat for the teenagers in your parish or school, take a look at the different topics available in *Quick Takes Rituals and Retreats*. What meets the current needs of your kids? Where are they hurting? What issues are they facing? Choose on this basis.

Then note that each retreat begins with an outline of what to expect in that Retreat Plan, as well as a complete list of Materials and a convenient Advance Preparation Checklist. We have covered all the bases...including some pesky details that can easily slip through the cracks. Throughout the Retreat Plan you will be referred back to this Introduction for helps and tips on various elements of the retreats.

#### Recruit and Train Team Leaders

We designed the retreats in this book for team facilitation. Recruit both youth (from the group) and adults (from the broader parish) to assist the retreat coordinator in planning and implementing the retreat. When selecting retreat Team Members, develop a balanced team with a variety of personalities and talents. From the outset, clarify, in writing, your expectations of each Team Member.

How do you develop competent and confident Team Members? You train them. Training takes place in a series of meetings prior to the retreat, focusing on the following:
- building relationships among Team Members
- teaching small- and large-group facilitation skills
- teaching ways to lead prayer
- discussing adolescent faith development
- modeling ways to share the faith and tell stories
- practicing how to lead specific activities

Many young people demonstrate natural leadership abilities and, with training, can lead other young people better than some adults. Do not assume, however, that these young people "naturally" know how to lead retreat activities. Preparing them in advance will build skills and confidence, and increase the chances of a successful retreat.

One excellent resource for training peer ministers is *Lights for the World* by Lisa-Marie Calderone-Stewart (1995, St. Mary's Press, Winona, MN).

## Maintaining the Team
Throughout the retreat, meet periodically with Team Leaders. These Check-Ins and Team Meetings are important for several reasons:
- Team Members can let you, the retreat coordinator, know how participants are experiencing the retreat.
- With this "insider" information, you and the Team can adjust the Retreat Plan, if necessary.
- Team Members can voice concerns and frustrations—and share the joys—of their experience as leaders.

Keep the Team Check-Ins between sessions brief. They serve as a way to "take the pulse" of the retreat. Ask how the retreat is going, and if Team Members have any immediate questions or concerns.

At the conclusion of the retreat, take a bit more time to allow Team Members to talk about their overall experience of leading the retreat. For example, you could ask:
- What went well on the retreat?
- What would you adjust or change about the retreat?
- How was your experience of leading the retreat?
- Do you have any specific concerns about people or activities?

Conclude this final Team Meeting with a prayer or blessing.

## Witness Talks
Jesus often told his disciples to go out and tell others about their experiences with him. In doing so, they witnessed to his teachings and works. We, too, are called to witness Christ's presence in our lives. We come to know Christ through events such as births, deaths, celebrations, tragedies and religious experiences. We also know Christ in our relationships with family and friends, teachers and co-workers.

For all of these reasons, most of the retreats in this book incorporate a Witness Talk in the Retreat Plan. Witness Talks do two things:
- First, they encourage young people to stand before their peers and witness to their faith. This strengthens the faith of the person who shares as well as those who hear the story.
- Second, Witness Talks help participants get in touch with Christ's presence in their own lives, focusing their thoughts and freeing them to talk about their faith.

## Gather Supplies and Prepare the Environment
Begin gathering supplies several weeks before the retreat. Leaving this task to the last minute almost always causes frustration and guarantees that you will forget something. Use the Materials list at the beginning of the retreat when developing your supply list.

Prepare the environment prior to the retreat. Be creative! Ask Team Members to help you design an environment that is inviting and comfortable for young people. Again, do not wait until the last minute to do this. The environment should be set in advance so that Team Members are present to greet participants when they arrive.

## Adapt, Adjust and Be Creative!
Bring your own creativity and the talents of your Team to the retreats in this book. While the activities are effective if led as written,

variations might better meet the needs of your particular participants. Feel free to rearrange activities, substitute activities, shorten or lengthen activities as it fits your group and its mood. Take more time for quiet reflection, add in free-time, set aside time for singing —do what you need to do to make this a great experience for participants.

## Pray

Once the planning and preparations for the retreat are complete, take time to pray with your Team Leaders. Ask God to allow the Spirit to work in and among those gathered. Be open to surprises! Things rarely go exactly as planned, but that does not mean you were ineffective—it might mean that God had a greater plan!

## Name Tags

Wearing name tags on a retreat helps participants get to know one another. In addition, name tags greatly assist Team Leaders and other facilitators who may or may not know the names of group members.

Name tags can be as simple as adhesive labels purchased from an office supply store. (**Note:** If you use adhesive labels, be sure to have enough labels for young people to make one label per day of retreat!) Other options for name tags include:

- Ask participants to add to their name tags symbols that reflect the theme of the retreat or interests in their lives.
- Add markings on the name tags to denote small groups (numbers, symbols, letters or colors).
- Allow participants to make their own name tags out of construction paper. Be sure to have markers, glue and scissors on hand.
- Invite an artist to make a large picture relating to the retreat theme. Cut the picture into as many pieces as there will be participants, then use these pieces for participants' name tags. Distribute name tags and ask participants to keep track of them because they will be used later. At some point near the end of the retreat, invite the group to bring their name tags together and assemble the "puzzle."

## Team Introductions

At the outset of the retreat, ask Team Members briefly to introduce themselves. Introductions might include name, school, occupation, interests, preferred recreational activities and/or what they hope happens on the retreat. Keep these introductions *brief*; simply provide participants "snapshots" of who they can look to for leadership during the retreat.

If your group is small enough, you could invite participants to follow the introduction format modeled by Team Members. For a very large group, this could be tedious and might better be done in small groups.

## Rules

*Very important:* Set clear boundaries and expectations at the beginning of the retreat. Many churches, schools and retreat facilities have rules that are "givens," but it is always a good idea to remind people of these expectations.

Rules are meant to help a group exist harmoniously with each other during the retreat. Young people often resist the retreat if they feel that they cannot move without breaking a rule, so only set *essential* rules. For assistance, invite your Team Members to come up with a list that you will review and add to, if necessary.

Some basic rules might include:
- no illegal drugs, alcohol or tobacco
- no weapons of any kind
- participants must remain on the property
- respect the facility and the personal property of other participants
- attend all sessions, unless excused by a Team Member
- listen to one another and Team Members with respect

Provide the rules for participants and their parents ahead of time. You might even want to include copies of the rules with the permission slips. As a reminder, review the rules at the beginning of the retreat.

Consequences for breaking the rules must also be clear. As the facilitator, stick to the rules and the consequences. For example, if the consequence for using alcohol is that a parent will be called and that young person well be sent home immediately, you must be willing to call a parent at 3 a.m. if that is when you discover a young person drinking.

## Overview of the Day

Today's typical young person lives a very busy and scheduled life. Many of them are so used to being "programmed" that they don't know how to "retreat." At the beginning of the retreat, help participants feel more comfortable by offering a general idea of what is ahead for the day or weekend. General comments might include:
- You will sometimes meet in large groups, sometimes in small groups.
- We will eat at these times...
- Bedtime is... We wake up around...
- The theme of this retreat is... Our hope for the retreat is...

## Journal Reflections

Most of the retreats in this book suggest a period of time when participants can write their thoughts on journal pages. This reflection process offers those who are more introverted or quiet a time to gather their thoughts. It can help those who are very vocal and talkative to take a few minutes to quiet down and listen to their inner thoughts.

Journal Reflections can serve as great discussion starters. If appropriate, invite, but do not force participants to share their reflections in large or small groups.

The journal sheets themselves are photocopiable and found at the back of the book, pages 101-113. You have permission to photocopy as many as you need.

## Evaluations

At the conclusion of the retreat, ask participants for brief, honest and specific feedback to keep you in tune with which activities do or do not work well with your group. If used, this information can be invaluable in your planning process for future retreats.

If you ask for evaluations, be sure to review and incorporate appropriate suggestions into future retreats. A caution when reviewing evaluations: It is often easy for one negative comment to speak louder than ten positive comments; don't throw out an activity because one person had a bad experience. Look at the *overall* comments and draw conclusions accordingly.

A sample evaluation form is included at the back of the book, page 114. You have permission to photocopy as many as you need.

## Departure

The retreats in this book suggest concluding the experience with a Closing Ritual. In addition to the rituals suggested, it might be helpful to offer a few suggestions to young people as they "reenter" their normal lives after a period of retreating. This is especially important if the retreat has included one or more nights away:
- Encourage participants to talk with family and friends about the retreat...to bear witness to what they experienced.
- Remind participants that not everyone has been away on retreat. They might be returning to their families and friends with new insights about themselves or others. Their friends and families, however, have not been on retreat and may not share their new insights and enthusiasm. Encourage participants to be patient if others do not immediately understand.
- Ask participants how they might continue the retreat experience once they have left. Encourage them to take initiative.

Finally, remind participants about confidentiality, namely, that the specifics of what people shared on the retreat should not be repeated to others outside of the retreat experience.

# THE RITUALS

## Linking Heart and Church

Rituals connect our personal, often intense experience of God with the greater Church—with the people who make up the Church, with the traditions of the Church, and with the familiar patterns of the Church's liturgy. Rituals provide experiences that are at once both inward and outward, both here-and-now and eternal, both individual and communal. Thus, rituals bridge all aspects of our life of faith.

These retreats include rituals for these same reasons: through sometimes familiar and sometimes fresh language and gesture, they link the discussions and activities of the retreats to the sweep of Church history, the panoramic scope of God's work. While affirming the uniqueness of our encounter with God, they assure us that we share this encounter with others at all times and around the globe.

We have set a pattern to the rituals in this book, a rhythm which, if the rituals are used on a regular basis, will become familiar to participants. As suggested above, in creating these rituals, we borrowed elements already familiar to those involved in the life and ritual of the Church.

## Preparing for the Rituals

Begin by reviewing the list of needed *materials* and gather what you need. This list appears at the beginning of each retreat. Note that we have listed materials for the ritual separately, in case you use the ritual in a setting other than the retreat.

Although written by a Catholic, the rituals can be used and adapted for ecumenical settings.

None of these rituals includes a Eucharistic celebration (Holy Communion). If celebrating Eucharist, consult with the presider to see if any portions of the ritual—especially those clearly linked to the retreat—could be incorporated into the Eucharist. Many of the penitential rites, litanies, ritual actions and blessings in the rituals are based on Catholic prayer, making such adaptation possible. Ritual actions, for example, could take place after the homily and before the profession of faith and/or prayers of the faithful.

Use *music* to gather the assembly. Quiet recorded or live music helps set the mood, focus participants and introduce the theme of the ritual. See "Music" later in the Introduction (page 6).

The presider (leader of prayer) can use the first moments of the ritual to further prepare participants. For example, consider beginning with a penitential rite, or, if the presider is joining the retreat at this time, he or she may ask what participants have experienced thus far, what they have felt, thought, learned or experienced.

Each ritual includes the reading of *scripture*. We usually take scripture readings from an activity used in the retreat, and therefore from the corresponding volume of *Quick Takes for Teens*, thus reinforcing the Word of God experienced in the retreat. A *psalm* follows the scripture reading—the act of the assembly letting human emotion respond to the Word of God. We recommend that the psalm always be sung.

The *reflection* is a time for the presider (leader of prayer) to break open the Word of God. The Advance Preparation Checklist, found at the beginning of each retreat, offers questions for the presider to use as he or she prepares the reflection; one or more of the questions could be included in the reflection for participants to consider.

Prepare well for the *ritual action*. Practice it, when possible, since it will be the one part of the ritual least familiar to Church rubrics. Adapt it; nuance it; know the assembly and trust the process.

In each ritual, the *litany* flows from the ritual action, and therefore changes in tone from penitential to petitionary to celebratory. The litany always concludes with the *Lord's Prayer* and a *blessing*.

The ritual ends with a *sign of peace* and is then followed by the *closing song*.

## Basic Premises of the Rituals
### Ministries

In any ritual or liturgy, who is the primary minister? *The assembly*. We often forget this; we try to find "things" for the assembly to do. They already have something to do: they bring their presence; they participate; they *do* the ritual, supported by all other ministries. Other ministers are servants of the assembly.

### Presider

The presider (leader of prayer) ideally would be a lay person of the community. Although this could be an ordained presbyter, it does not have to be. It should, however, be a single leader. To move the role from person to person because you want to "give everyone a chance" dilutes the power of this ministry. Find someone who feels comfortable in front of a large group, gestures easily and can communicate the awe and wonder of the ritual. Feel free to seek members of the community who have these qualities and ask them to help with the rituals.

### Readers

In most cases throughout these rituals, we list the presider as the sole leader. Additional people, well-prepared, can of course participate as lectors (readers of scripture). Again, choose readers based on their ability to do the task, not from the need to give everyone an opportunity to do something. When proclaiming scripture, read from a lectionary or Bible, not from a sheet of paper. Mark your readings and have them ready for the reader to rehearse.

### The Environment

Recognize the importance of the environment for prayer. Is there room in the retreat facility to set aside a special place dedicated to the ritual? Besides the materials listed for each ritual (at the beginning of each retreat), consider also displaying a cross, some candles (lightly scented ones work well), an incense bowl and some fabric or draping that lets the retreatants know they are in a holy place. The parish art and environment committees might suggest other ideas. During sessions outside of Lent, include fresh flowers, plants and a bowl of water. During Lent, use bundles of bare branches warmed by the glow of candlelight—a more solemn, austere look.

### Music

Music is integral to each ritual. To not sing would be like saying the words "Happy Birthday" and not singing them; the impact would be lost.

We always offer more than one suggestion for music, understanding that parishes differ in the number and variety of available resources. Even, so, the songs we recommend are suggestions only; choose what you know works best with your participants, making sure it is singable for those present. Recruit a song leader with experience in animating an assembly and calling people into song. The addition of one or more instrumentalists—including a percussionist—adds greatly to the power of the music. If necessary, play recorded music for background or to teach new songs to the assembly.

The music suggested in the rituals comes from the publishers listed below. Contact them for further information.

Oregon Catholic Press (OCP)
5536 NE Hassalo
Portland, OR 97213
1-800-LITURGY (548-8749) or 503/281-1191
http://www.liturgy.com

GIA Publications, Inc.
7404 South Mason Avenue
Chicago, IL 60638
(800) GIA-1358 (442-1358) or (708) 496-3800
Fax: (708) 496-3828
http://www.giamusic.com
E-mail: custserv-giamusic.com

A word about Taizé Music: Taizé is an ecumenical community in France, founded in 1940 by brothers of different Protestant denominations. Today it includes many Catholics. Since 1960 it has attracted young people ages 18-30 who come for pilgrimages and times of prayer. During World Youth Day 1998 in Paris, many American youth visited Taizé as part of their holy tour. Taizé offers a powerful form of prayer for youth. GIA Publications distributes Taizé materials in the U.S. More information on this community and their offerings can be found at the GIA website (*www.giamusic.com*) and at the Taizé website (*www.taize.fr*).

## Using the Rituals with the Overnight Retreats

Each of the overnight retreats (#s 4, 8, 12 and 16) concludes with a Closing Ritual. You are encouraged to choose a ritual from those offered in the previous three retreats, depending on the needs and interests of retreatants.

Each overnight retreat also includes time for Compline and Morning Prayer. We suggest two options at these times:

- Adapt another of the rituals from one of the three previous retreats.
- Use the Liturgy of the Hours as appropriate. The Liturgy of the Hours requires a strong presider and, because of the amount of singing, a strong cantor. Increase the meaning of these prayers by limiting the words and relying on visual imagery — gestures, candles and incense. A helpful resource is *Praise God in Song* by Storey, Melloh, Hughes, Isele and Joncas (GIA), with settings and music for Morning Prayer, Evening Prayer and Compline. See also "The Liturgy of the Hours" in *Worship* (GIA) and "Daily Prayer" in *Gather* (GIA) for further guidelines.

Here are basic patterns for these three prayers:

*Morning Prayer*
(celebrated from sunrise through midmorning)

Invitatory (O Lord Open my Lips)
Opening Hymn
Psalmody (often Psalm 63)
Psalm Prayer
Scripture
Silence
Canticle of Zachary
Litany
Lord's Prayer
Concluding Prayer
Blessing and Dismissal
Sign of Peace

*Evening Prayer*
(celebrated at sundown through early evening)

Invitatory (Light and Peace in Jesus Christ our Lord)
Evening Hymn
Psalmody (often Psalm 141 with use of incense)
Psalm Prayer
Scripture
Silence
Canticle of Mary (Magnificat)
Litany
Lord's Prayer
Concluding Prayer
Blessing and Dismissal
Sign of Peace

*Compline*
(celebrated late at night)

Invitatory
Night Hymn
Examination of Conscience or extended Penitential Rite
Psalmody (often Psalm 4)
Psalm Prayer
Scripture
Silence
Canticle of Simeon (Nunc Dimittis)
Litany
Lord's Prayer
Closing Prayer
Concluding Rite and blessing
Hymn to Mary (Salve Regina)

# CHAPTER 1

## RETREAT #1:
### CONFLICT IN THE FAMILY: FROM LOSE/LOSE TO WIN/WIN

## GETTING READY

### Focus
Retreat #1 examines family conflict. Participants explore ways in which they handle family conflict and practice healthy options for conflict resolution.

### Core Questions
- What is conflict?
- When and where do we experience conflict?
- How do our families deal with conflict?
- How do we handle conflict?
- In what ways can careful listening and improved communication reduce conflict?

### Overview
| | |
|---|---|
| 8:00 am | Team Arrives for Set-Up and Team Meeting |
| 9:00 am | Participants Arrive |
| 9:15 am | Welcome: Team Introductions, Rules and Overview of the Day |
| 9:30 am | Session 1: Community Building |
| 10:15 am | Snack Break and Team Check-In |
| 10:30 am | Session 2: Defining Conflict |
| 11:30 am | Lunch and Team Check-In |
| 12:15 pm | Session 3: Conflict in Families |
| 1:15 pm | Session 4: Listening and Communication Skills |
| 2:00 pm | Closing Ritual: Making Peace |
| 2:25 pm | Evaluation |
| 2:30 pm | Departure and Team Meeting |

### Materials
*for the retreat:*
- copies of *Quick Takes for Teens*, Volume 1, 1 per Team Leader
- Bibles
- name-tag supplies
- newsprint
- colored felt markers
- masking tape
- CD player
- CDs appropriate for breaks and reflection times
- photocopies of Journal #1 (page 101), 1 per participant
- photocopies of the Evaluation (page 114), 1 per participant
- pens or pencils
- index cards
- stopwatch or watch with second hand
- food and beverages for breaks and lunch

*for the ritual:*
- 1 or more clay pots filled with sand
- taper candles, 1 per participant
- paper wax catchers, 1 per participant
- matches
- recorded or printed music:
  — "Prayer for Peace" by David Haas (GIA) or "Out of Darkness" by Tom Kendzia (OCP)
  — a musical setting of Psalm 27 that is familiar to your community
  — "The Lord Is My Light" (Taizé, distributed in the U.S. by GIA) or "We Are the Light of the World" by Steve Agrisano (OCP)

- cross
- small basket for paper wax catchers

## Advance Preparation Checklist

- ☐ Set the date and reserve the site. Check both school and parish calendars!
- ☐ Read through the Retreat Plan. Decide which activities to include, substitute, adapt, etc.
- ☐ Recruit and train the Retreat Team. See page 1 of the Introduction.
- ☐ Recruit a Team Member to give the Witness Talk in Session 3. Besides the basic guidelines given in the Introduction (page 2), suggest to the Team Member:
  — In your talk, reflect on 1 Peter 3:9-12.
  — Share about a specific family conflict, how you handled it and how it was resolved.
- ☐ Decide who will preside at the Closing Ritual. Ask the presider to prepare the Reflection to be given in the ritual. In the Reflection, the presider shares thoughts on conflict and peace-making. The following questions may help in preparation:
  — When and where in life do you experience conflict?
  — At these times, where (or to whom) do you turn to find peace?
  — What *interior* obstacles keep you from confronting your conflicts with others?
  — In what ways have you experienced the peace of Christ in your own life?
  — Who in your life is an example of God's peace?

  As a part of the Reflection, the presider may wish to have the assembly reflect on any one of these same questions, either silently or in groups of no more than three members each.
- ☐ Arrange for food and beverages.
- ☐ Arrange for transportation, as necessary.
- ☐ Get permission slips, as necessary.
- ☐ Photocopy necessary materials, for example, Journal Sheets and Evaluations.
- ☐ Collect and pack materials.
- ☐ Envision the environment and prepare necessary materials. See the Introduction, page 2.
- ☐ Pre-assign participants to small groups. Assign a Team Member to facilitate each group. Determine locations for small-group discussions.

## RETREAT PLAN

**8:00 am** Team Arrives for Set-Up and Team Meeting
See the Introduction, page 2.

**9:00 am** Participants Arrive

**Name Tags**
See the Introduction, page 3.

**9:15 am** Welcome
See the Introduction, pages 3-4.

**Team Introductions**
*(5 minutes)*

**Rules**
*(5 minutes)*

**Overview of the Day**
*(5 minutes)*

**9:30 am** Session 1: Community Building

We suggest the following icebreakers. Add your favorites or choose others from *Quick Takes for Teens*, Volume 1, pages 6-7.

**Introductions**
*(15 minutes)*
See *Quick Takes for Teens Volume 1*, page 7.

**My Ideal**
*(15 minutes)*
See *Quick Takes for Teens Volume 1*, page 6.

**10:15 am** Snack Break and Team Check-In
See the Introduction, page 2.

**10:30 am** Session 2: Defining Conflict

### Who Gets a Chair?
*(30 minutes)*
See *Quick Takes for Teens*, Volume 1, page 9.

At the conclusion of "Who Gets a Chair?" invite participants to brainstorm different types of conflict. Record their suggestions on newsprint. Examples could include specific issues of conflict within families, friendships, the world, religions, political structures, nature, etc.

After compiling the list, discuss:
- How does conflict start?
- What feelings add to conflict? *(fear, loss, competition, jealousy, etc.)*
- What words describe the end of conflict? *(peace, serenity, joy, love, etc.)*

### Journal Reflection
*(30 minutes)*
Distribute pens or pencils, Bibles and photocopies of Journal #1. Invite participants to work individually to complete this sheet.

After about 5 minutes, divide participants into smaller groups of 7-9 members each. Invite small groups to share their journal reflections with each other.

**11:30 am** Lunch and Team Check-In
See the Introduction, page 2.

**12:15 pm** Session 3: Conflict in Families

Regather the group, refocus their attention and introduce the Witness Talk Team Member.

### Witness Talk
*(10 minutes)*
See the Introduction, page 2, and the Advance Preparation Checklist, above.

### A Bag of Pressure
*(25 minutes)*
See *Quick Takes for Teens*, Volume 1, page 13.

Introduce this activity by inviting participants to return to the small groups of the previous session, then explaining that all members will now have an opportunity to explore how conflict surfaces in their own families. Distribute index cards to all participants. Make sure they all also have pens or pencils.

### Changing Things
*(20 minutes)*
See *Quick Takes for Teens*, Volume 1, page 13.

Regather participants; conduct this activity in the *large* group.

### Stretch Break
*(5 minutes)*
Give group members a brief break while you prepare for the next session.

**1:15 pm** Session 4: Listening and Communication Skills

### Yes/No
*(15 minutes)*
Share the following, in these or your own words:
- In this session, we explore ways in which we communicate with each other. Some ways are helpful; others are not.
- Let's see if we can learn new ways of communicating by sharing what is inside of us, rather than attacking what we imagine is in the other person.

Offer these directions to group members:
- Find a partner. Sit face to face with your partner.
- With your partner, decide which of you will be *the parent* and which will be *the teenager*.
- Now, for the next 15 second, *the parent* will say the word *no* repeatedly, and only the word *no*. Meanwhile, *the teenager* will say the word *yes* repeatedly, but only the word *yes*.
- Are you ready? On your mark, get set, go!

After 15 seconds, stop participants and switch the scenario as suggested below. There are five more rounds, each of which lasts 15 seconds:
- Round 2: *The parent* continues to say *no*. *The teenager* continues to say *yes*. *The parent*, however, *stands up*.
- Round 3: *The parent* continues to say *no*. *The teenager* continue to say *yes*. This time, however, *the parent sits down* and *the teenager stands up*. Remind partners of their parent and teenager roles.
- Round 4: *The parent* remains seated. *The teenager* remains standing. This time, *the parent* says *yes* and *the teenager* says *no*.
- Round 5: Both *the parent* and *the teenager stand up*. *The parent* continues to say *yes* and *the teenager* continues to say *no*. Once again remind partners of their parent and teenager roles.
- Round 6: Both *the parent* and *the teenager* remain *standing* and both say *yes*.

Invite participants to be seated and discuss:
- As you participated, what, in *your* mind, were you arguing about?
- As the rounds progressed, what did you notice about the way you felt?
- What were you wanting to say that you couldn't?
- How did you feel being at different levels? the same level?
- What does this activity illustrate about how we interact with our parents?
- In what way does "being on the same level" with our parents or other family members help communication?

**Practice!**
*(30 minutes)*
See *Quick Takes for Teens*, Volume 1, page 14.
Introduce this activity by saying:
- Good listening is critical for both preventing and resolving conflict.
- Let's see what we learn about these important skills in this activity.

# Ritual

**2:00 pm** Closing Ritual: Making Peace
Begin by distributing candles and wax catchers.

**Gathering Song**
Sing together "Prayer for Peace" or "Out of Darkness."

**Introductory Rite**
*Presider:*
In the name of the Father, and of the Son and of the Holy Spirit.

*All:*
Amen.

*Presider:*
> The peace of the Lord be with you.

*All:*
> And also with you.

*Presider:*
> As we come to the end of this time, we are called to celebrate the fact that we can name our conflicts. We turn to God and ask God to help us forgive, to help us find peace in our own lives. Christ is the light of the World. Let us now open our hearts and minds to the light of Christ.
>
> *Let us pray. (silence)*
>
> God of light and peace, your Son Jesus gave us the gift of peace as a sign of your love for us. Help us to face conflicts in our lives and to turn to you for strength and guidance. May our actions each day praise you as the God who lives and reigns forever and ever.

*All:*
> Amen.

## Scripture
All stand for the reading of the gospel.

*Reader:*
> The Lord be with you.

*All:*
> And also with you.

*Reader:*
> A reading from the holy gospel according to John.

*All:*
> Glory to you, Lord.

Read John 14:27.

*Presider:*
> The gospel of the Lord.

*All:*
> Praise to you, Lord Jesus Christ.

## Psalm
Sing a setting of Psalm 27.

## Reflection
The presider shares a few thoughts on resolving conflict, making peace and experiencing forgiveness. See the Introduction, page 5, and the Advance Preparation Checklist, above.

## Ritual Action
Begin by singing together "The Lord Is My Light" or "We Are the Light of the World."

Light the candles, inviting the assembly to pass the flame from candle to candle.

When all candles have been lit, continue with the Litany of Conflict and Peace.

## Litany of Conflict and Peace
*Presider:*
> As people of light, let us name those areas in our lives that need the light of Christ. *(If you wish, write your own invocations based on issues brought up during the retreat, substituting them for those offered here.)*
>
> For the darkness in our relationships with our families, may their be light in all our hearts. Let us pray to the Lord.

*All:*
> Lord, hear our prayer.

*Presider:*
> For the darkness in our relationships with our friends, may the light of peace fill our hearts. Let us pray to the Lord.

*All:*
> Lord, hear our prayer.

*Presider:*
> For the darkness clouding our own self-images, may the light of acceptance fill our hearts. Let us pray to the Lord.

*All:*
> Lord, hear our prayer.

*Presider:*
> For the darkness found in our insensitivity to the needs of the greater community, may the light of justice fill our hearts. Let us pray to the Lord.

*All:*
> Lord, hear our prayer.

*Presider:*
> For the darkness that keeps us from facing conflict, may the light of resolution fill our hearts. Let us pray to the Lord.

*All:*
> Lord, hear our prayer.

*Presider:*
> We are all lights of God's love. Together we can help one another resolve conflicts. Let us come forward, praising God, placing our candles at the foot of the cross.

Begin singing an alleluia or another hymn of praise. During this song, participants come forward to place their candles in the clay pots, *after first removing the paper wax catchers.* Participants can place their wax catchers in the basket. You may want to have a person at each clay pot arranging candles, moving as many to the center of the pots as possible. After all candles are in the clay pots, observe a period of silence.

After the silence, the presider asks everyone to stand and pray.

**Concluding Rite**

*Presider:*
> Let us pray in the words Christ gave us:

*All:*
> Our Father... Amen.

*Presider:*
> The Lord be with you.

*All:*
> And also with you.

*Presider:*
> God of everlasting love, you loved us enough to give us Jesus as a gift of peace. May our actions always be ones of peace and love. We praise you as the God who lives and reigns forever and ever, and may you bless us, Father, Son and Holy Spirit.

*All:*
> Amen.

*Presider:*
> Let us go forth to love and serve our God and one another.

*All:*
> Thanks be to God.

Begin playing music for reprise of "Prayer for Peace" or "Out of Darkness."

*Presider:*
    Let us offer each other a sign of God's peace.

The music continues as participants exchange a Sign of Peace.

Ask a volunteer to extinguish the candles.

When everyone has been greeted, conclude by singing "Prayer for Peace" or "Out of Darkness."

**2:25 pm**   Evaluation
           See the Introduction, page 4.

**2:30 pm**   Departure and Team Meeting
           See the Introduction, pages 2 and 4.

# RETREAT #2:
## Understanding Parents

### GETTING READY

#### Focus
Retreat #2 offers young people the opportunity to examine their relationships with parents—both the good and the bad! Participants explore their "family history," share the current status of their relationships with their parents and look for ways to improve these relationships.

**Note:** Throughout the retreat, be aware that group members come from both single- and dual-parent homes, as well as a variety of blended families. As necessary, adapt questions to reflect this reality; for example, at times it may be more appropriate to ask, "How does this reflect your relationship with your *parent*" (singular) than "How does this reflect your relationship to your *parents*" (plural).

#### Core Questions
- What's the nature of our families?
- How well do we communicate with our parents?
- What issues are current in our relationships to our parents?
- How can we improve our relationships with our parents?
- What part does God play in our relationships with our parents?

#### Overview
| | |
|---|---|
| 8:00 am | Team Arrives for Set-Up and Team Meeting |
| 9:00 am | Participants Arrive |
| 9:15 am | Welcome: Team Introductions, Rules and Overview of the Day |
| 9:30 am | Session 1: Community Building |
| 10:15 am | Snack Break and Team Check-In |
| 10:30 am | Session 2: Family Roots |
| 11:30 am | Lunch and Team Check-In |
| 12:15 pm | Session 3: Understanding Parents |
| 1:15 pm | Session 4: The View from the Other Side |
| 2:00 pm | Closing Ritual: Celebrating Our Roots |
| 2:30 pm | Departure and Team Meeting |

#### Materials
*for the retreat:*
- copies of *Quick Takes for Teens*, Volume 1, 1 per Team Leader
- Bibles
- name-tag supplies
- paper
- pens or pencils
- index cards
- safety pins or masking tape
- colored construction paper
- newsprint
- colored felt markers
- masking tape
- CD player
- CDs appropriate for breaks and reflection times
- photocopies of Journal #2 (page 102), 1 per participant
- photocopies of the Evaluation (page 114), 1 per participant
- food and beverages for breaks and lunch

*for the ritual:*
- photographs of participants' parents, grandparents and other older relatives

- recorded or printed music:
  - "Gathered in the Love of Christ" by Marty Haugen (GIA) or "Malo! Malo! Thanks Be to God" by Jesse Manibusan (OCP)
  - "Covenant Hymn" by Gary Daigle and Rory Cooney (GIA) or "One Love" by Bob Marley, as recorded by Tom Booth on the CD "Tom Booth" (OCP)
  - a musical setting of Psalm 100 that is familiar to your community
- a table set with:
  - cloth covering several different levels of wood blocks
  - flowers
  - candles
  - small blank book and pen
  - matches

## Advance Preparation Checklist

- [ ] Set the date and reserve the site. Check both school and parish calendars!
- [ ] Read through the Retreat Plan. Decide which activities to include, substitute, adapt, etc.
- [ ] Recruit and train the Retreat Team. See page 1 of the Introduction.
- [ ] Recruit a Team Member to give the Witness Talk in Session 3. Besides the basic guidelines given in the Introduction (page 2), you might also suggest to the Team Member:
  - In your talk, reflect on Ephesians 6:1-4.
  - Share an example of your own experiences—both good and bad—communicating with your parents.
- [ ] Decide who will preside at the Closing Ritual Ask the presider to prepare the Reflection to be given in the ritual. In the Reflection, the presider shares thoughts on parents and families. The following questions may help in preparation:
  - How have your parents (grandparents, etc.) shown you the love of God? How have they helped you grow spiritually?
  - Describe a time when you became upset with your parents (grandparents, etc.) because of their "beliefs." How have you resolved this in your own life?
  - In what ways is God a "parent" to you in your spiritual life?

As a part of the Reflection, the presider may wish to have the assembly reflect on any one of these same questions, either silently or in groups of no more than three members each.

- [ ] Arrange for food and beverages.
- [ ] Arrange for transportation, as necessary.
- [ ] Get permission slips, as necessary.
- [ ] Photocopy necessary materials, for example, Journal Sheets and Evaluations.
- [ ] Arrange for each participant to bring several photographs of their parents, grandparents or other older relatives.
- [ ] Copy onto poster board the quotes found in "Quote Parents Unquote," *Quick Takes for Teens*, Volume 1, page 37. You won't be using the activity, but the quotes offer food for thought throughout the retreat.
- [ ] Collect and pack materials.
- [ ] Envision the environment and prepare necessary materials. See the Introduction, page 3.
- [ ] Pre-assign participants to small groups. Assign a Team Member to facilitate each group. Determine locations for small-group discussions.

# RETREAT PLAN

**8:00 am** Team Arrives for Set-Up and Team Meeting
See the Introduction, page 2.

**9:00 am** Participants Arrive

**Name Tags**
See the Introduction, page 3.

**9:15 am** Welcome
See the Introduction, pages 3-4.

**Team Introductions**
(5 minutes)

**Rules**
(5 minutes)

**Overview of the Day**
(5 minutes)

**9:30 am** Session 1: Community Building
We suggest the following icebreakers. Add your favorites or choose others from *Quick Takes for Teens*, Volume 1, pages 6-7.

### Family Roles
*(20 minutes)*
See *Quick Takes for Teens*, Volume 1, page 26.

### Mother/Father Says
*(20 minutes)*
See *Quick Takes for Teens*, Volume 1, page 39.

**10:15 am** Snack Break and Team Check-In
See the Introduction, page 2.

**10:30 am** Session 2: Family Roots

### Family Stories
*(20 minutes)*
Invite participants to share stories about their grandparents. After all who wish to share a story have done so, discuss:
- What do you imagine life was like for our grandparents when *they* were teenagers? How might their teenage years have been similar to ours? different?

### Journal Reflection
*(20 minutes)*
Distribute pens or pencils and copies of Journal #2. Invite group members to work individually to complete this sheet.

After 10 minutes of journal reflection, divide participants into smaller groups of 7-9 members each. Ask group members to share their reflections with each other.

### Inheritance
*(20 minutes)*
See *Quick Takes for Teens*, Volume 1, page 31.

Regather the large group for this activity. In particular, focus on the questions after the second bullet, which stress how families "hand down" ways of relating from generation to generation.

**11:30 am** Lunch and Team Check-In
See the Introduction, page 2.

**12:15 pm** Session 3: Understanding Parents

### Communicating with Parents
*(20 minutes)*
See *Quick Takes for Teens*, Volume 1, page 12.

### Witness Talk
*(10 minutes)*
See the Introduction, page 2, and the Advance Preparation Checklist, above.

### Freeze Frames
*(25 minutes)*
See *Quick Takes for Teens*, Volume 1, page 30.

As written in *Quick Takes*, this activity invites group members to pose scenes that reflect dynamics in their families. As you use the activity here, however, ask group members to pose a scene that specifically shows their relationship *with their parents*. If other family members appear in the scenes, that's fine, but be certain that they also echo the relationship of teens *with parents*. Model the activity for group members first, and let them know that they may pose any issue they currently have with their parents. Some of these issues may be painful; be prepared to identify and facilitate their expression.

Conclude the activity by discussing:
- What parent/teen issues surfaced in this activity?
- How many of these are current issues for others of us in the group?
- What similarities to these scenes do you see in your own family? What differences?
- How do you deal with these issues with *your* parents?

### Stretch Break
*(5 minutes)*
Give group members a brief break while you prepare for the next session.

**1:15 pm** Session 4: The View from the Other Side

### Differences
*(15 minutes)*
See *Quick Takes for Teens*, Volume 1, page 39.

### Fast Forward
*(15 minutes)*
See *Quick Takes for Teens*, Volume 1, page 28.

At the conclusion of the activity, discuss:
- You've just discovered what kind of parent you hope to be.
- To what extent have your parents (has your parent) tried to be this kind of parent for you?

### You Are Your Parent
*(15 minutes)*
See *Quick Takes for Teens*, Volume 1, page 33.

Conclude the activity by discussing:
- What have you learned today about your parent(s)?
- What have you learned today about yourself?
- What have you learned today about your relationship with your parent(s)?

# Ritual

**2:00 pm** Closing Ritual: Celebrating Our Roots

### Gathering Song
Sing together "Gathered in the Love of Christ" or "Malo! Malo! Thanks Be to God."

### Introductory Rite
*Presider:*
In the name of the Father, Son and Holy Spirit.

*All:*
Amen.

*Presider:*
The Lord be with you.

*All:*
And also with you.

*Presider:*
We all have parents. As unique as each of *us* are, so are each of our parents, each with his or her unique dreams and fears, hopes and hurts, happy memories, painful history. Today we acknowledge what is painful in our relationships with our parents and families, while at the same time remembering and celebrating what is good about those relationships. We recognize all — for good or ill — that our parents, grandparents and ancestors have contributed to our personal stories.

### Opening Prayer
*Presider:*
Let us pray. *(silence)*

God, who loves us a parent loves a child, you taught us to love through the example of Mary and Joseph. May we be open to your love as expressed in our relationships with our families. We ask this through Christ our Lord.

*All:*
Amen.

### Scripture
*Reader:*
A reading from the book of Proverbs.

Read Proverbs 3:1-6.

*Reader:*
> The word of the Lord.

*All:*
> Thanks be to God.

**Psalm**
Sing a setting of Psalm 100.

**Reflection**
Presider shares a few comments on parents and families. See the Introduction, page 5, and the Advance Preparation Checklist, above.

**Ritual Action**

*Presider:*
> We gather today, recognizing that we have all come from different parents and grandparents, yet we all together make up the body of Christ. Let us bring forward images of those who have been "parents" in our lives.

Sing together selected verses of "Covenant Hymn" or "One Love." As participants sing, they bring forward their photographs of parents, grandparents, etc. and place them on the table prepared before the session. Those who have not brought photographs to the session may write in the blank book the names of people who have "parented" them throughout their lives. (Those with photographs may do the same, if they wish.)

Continue playing music as the presider continues:

*Presider:*
> Gathering in the presence of these images and names, let us offer to God our prayers of this day.
>
> For all who have shown us love, let us pray to the Lord.

*All:*
> Lord, hear our prayer.

*Presider:*
> For parents, grandparents and ancestors who have shared faith with us, let us pray to the Lord.

*All:*
> Lord, hear our prayer.

*Presider:*
> For all who struggle in the commitment of parenting, let us pray to the Lord.

*All:*
> Lord, hear our prayer.

*Presider:*
> For all the hurts and struggles within our families— especially with our parents, let us pray to the Lord.

*All:*
> Lord, hear our prayer.

*Presider:*
> For those we know who are ill and struggle with life, let us pray to the Lord.

*All:*
> Lord, hear our prayer.

*Presider:*
> For those who have died and have gone before us to enjoy the table of eternal life, let us pray to the Lord.

*All:*
> Lord, hear our prayer.

Sing selected verses of "Covenant Hymn" or "One Love."

*Presider:*
Remembering those who have parented us, let us ask God's blessing upon them:

Holy and gracious God, we humbly pray for those who have been called to be parents. May they rejoice together in your gift of parenting.

May all parents praise you when they are happy and turn to you in their sorrows. May our parents be glad that you help them in their work and know you are with them in their need. May they pray to you in the community of the Church, and may they be your witnesses in the world. May our parents reach old age in the company of their friends, and may those who have gone before live forever in the kingdom of heaven. We pray this through Christ our Lord.*

*All:*
Amen.

Sing selected verses of "Covenant Hymn" or "One Love."

**Concluding Rite**

*Presider:*
Let us pray in the words Christ gave us:

*All:*
Our Father... Amen.

*Presider:*
The Lord be with you.

*All:*
And also with you.

*Presider:*
Let us pray:

Loving and faithful God, you call us to never forget your teachings and always let our hearts live your commandments. May we always be loyal and faithful to our parents, grandparents and ancestors, whose stories have formed the story of our lives. May we recognize your goodness and kindness in their actions and words. And may you bless us, Father, Son and Holy Spirit.

*All:*
Amen.

*Presider:*
Let us go forth to love and serve our God and one another.

*All:*
Thanks be to God.

Invite group members to exchange a Sign of Peace.

**Concluding Song**
Sing together "Gathered in the Love of Christ" or "Malo! Malo! Thanks Be to God."

**2:25 pm** Evaluation
See the Introduction, page 4.

**3:00 pm** Departure and Team Meeting
See the Introduction, pages 2 and 4.

*Prayer adapted from Nuptial Blessing #121 of Rite of Marriage.

# RETREAT #3:
## SURVIVING SIBLINGS

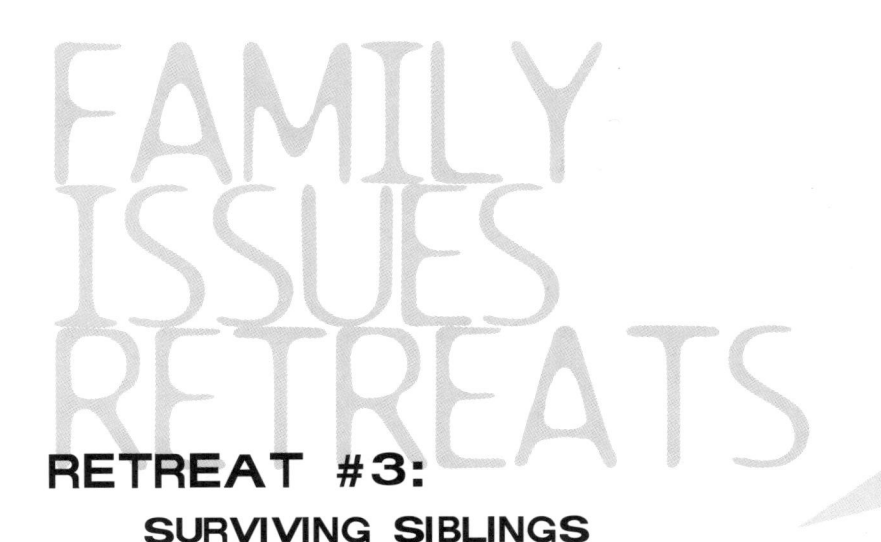

## GETTING READY

### Focus
Retreat #3 explores group members' relationships with their brothers and sisters. Participants examine the current status of such relationships, what causes conflicts with brothers and sisters, and how to get along better.

**Note:** Throughout this retreat, be aware that some young people may not have siblings. As necessary, adapt questions to reflect this reality. Some suggestions are made for you in the Retreat Plan.

### Core Questions
- What is sibling rivalry?
- In what ways do we contribute to both sibling rivalry and sibling harmony?
- What do we learn from scripture about getting along with our brothers and sisters?
- What practical steps can I take to improve my relationships with my brothers and sisters, or with friends with whom I have close, sibling-like relationships?

### Overview
| | |
|---|---|
| 8:00 am | Team Arrives for Set-Up and Team Meeting |
| 9:00 am | Participants Arrive |
| 9:15 am | Welcome: Team Introductions, Rules and Overview of the Day |
| 9:30 am | Session 1: Community Building |
| 10:15 am | Snack Break and Team Check-In |
| 10:30 am | Session 2: The Wacky World of Siblings |
| 11:30 am | Lunch and Team Check-In |
| 12:15 pm | Session 3: What Kind of Sibling Am I? |
| 1:15 pm | Session 4: What Kind of Sibling Do I Want To Be? |
| 2:00 pm | Closing Ritual: Celebrating the Gift of Brothers and Sisters |
| 2:25 pm | Evaluation |
| 2:30 pm | Departure and Team Meeting |

### Materials
*for the retreat:*
- copies of *Quick Takes for Teens*, Volume 1, 1 per Team Member
- Bibles
- name-tag supplies
- newsprint
- colored felt markers
- masking tape
- 2 chairs
- paper
- pens or pencils
- CD player
- CDs appropriate for breaks and reflection times
- photocopies of The Prodigal Story (page 115), 1 per participant
- photocopies of Journal #3 (page 103), 1 per participant
- photocopies of the Evaluation (page 114), 1 per participant
- food and beverages for breaks and lunch

*for the ritual:*
- recorded or printed music:
  — "All Are Welcome" by Marty Haugen (GIA) or "Over My Head" as arranged by Tom Kendzia (OCP)

— a musical setting of Psalm 100 that is familiar to your community

## Advance Preparation Checklist

- [ ] Set the date and reserve the site. Check both school and parish calendars!
- [ ] Read through the Retreat Plan. Decide which activities to include, substitute, adapt, etc.
- [ ] Recruit and train the Retreat Team. See the Introduction, page 1.
- [ ] Recruit a Team Member to give the Witness Talk in Session 3. Besides the basic guidelines given in the Introduction (page 2), suggest to the Team Member:
  — In your talk, reflect on Proverbs 17:17b.
  — Share about a time when a brother or sister—who normally may annoy you—helped you in a time of trouble or pain.
- [ ] Decide who will preside at the Closing Ritual. Ask the presider to prepare the Reflection to be given in the ritual. In the Reflection, the presider shares thoughts on siblings and improving relationships with them. The following questions may help in preparation:
  — What is special about the relationship you have with a sister or brother (even if he or she isn't your "flesh-and-blood" brother or sister)?
  — When have you had to confront a brother or sister? What was the result?
  — What unique gift do your bring to the relationship of brother or sister?

  As a part of the Reflection, the presider may wish to have the assembly reflect on any one of these same questions, either silently or in groups of no more than three members each.
- [ ] Arrange for food and beverages.
- [ ] Arrange for transportation, as necessary.
- [ ] Get permission slips, as necessary.
- [ ] Photocopy necessary materials, for example, Journal Sheets, Evaluations and The Prodigal Story.
- [ ] Collect and pack materials.
- [ ] Envision the environment and prepare necessary materials. See the Introduction, page 2.
- [ ] Pre-assign participants to small groups. Assign a Team Member to facilitate each group. Determine locations for small-group discussions.

## RETREAT PLAN

**8:00 am** Team Arrives for Set-Up and Team Meeting
See The Introduction, page 2.

**9:00 am** Participants Arrive

### Name Tags
See the Introduction, page 3.

**9:15 am** Welcome
See the Introduction, pages 3-4.

### Team Introductions
*(5 minutes)*

### Rules
*(5 minutes)*

### Overview of the Day
*(5 minutes)*

**9:30 am** Session 1: Community Building
We suggest the following icebreakers. Add your favorites or choose others from *Quick Takes for Teens*, Volume 1, pages 6-7.

### Open-Ended Statements
*(15 minutes)*
See *Quick Takes for Teens*, Volume 1, page 7.

### Sibling Songs
*(15 minutes)*
See *Quick Takes for Teens*, Volume 1, page 45.

**10:15 am** Snack Break and Team Check-In
See the Introduction, page 2.

**10:30 am** Session 2: The Wacky World of Siblings

### Compatible?
*(20 minutes)*
See *Quick Takes for Teens*, Volume 1, page 43.

The instructions for this activity suggest that you prepare and conduct a sibling survey *prior* to the meeting. Instead, *begin* the activity by informally conducting the survey, keeping track of the results on newsprint. Note that there are two parts to the survey, first, some general questions, and second, five items that group members rate on a scale of 1 (low) to 10 (high).

After the survey, discuss the three questions found at the end of the activity.

### The Prodigal Story
*(20 minutes)*
Distribute photocopies of The Prodigal Story (page 115), a dramatic reading based on Jesus' parable of the Prodigal Son in Luke 15:11-32. Recruit volunteers to read the parts of *the narrator, the younger child, the parent* and *the older child*. Observe that readers may improvise additions to their parts. Introduce the reading by saying:
- Here's a story that Jesus told about sibling relationships.

Ask the volunteers to read The Prodigal Story.

### Journal Reflection
*(20 minutes)*
Distribute pens or pencils, Bibles and photocopies of Journal #3. Invite participants to work individually to complete this sheet.

After about 5 minutes, divide participants into smaller groups of 7-9 members each. Invite small groups to share their journal reflections with each other.

**11:30 am** Lunch and Team Check-In
See the Introduction, page 2.

**12:15 pm** Session 3: What Kind of Sibling Am I?
Regather the group, refocus their attention and introduce the Witness Talk Team member.

### Witness Talk
*(10 minutes)*
See the Introduction, page 2, and the Advance Preparation Checklist, above.

### Real Dialogue
*(25 minutes)*
See *Quick Takes for Teens*, Volume 1, page 42.

### Parable Rewrite
*(20 minutes)*
See *Quick Takes for Teens*, Volume 1, page 43.

### Stretch Break
*(5 minutes)*
Give group members a brief break while you prepare for the next session.

**1:15 pm** Session 4: What Kind of Sibling Do I Want To Be?

### Bible Siblings
*(15 minutes)*
See *Quick Takes for Teens*, Volume 1, page 44.

### Ideal or Real?
*(15 minutes)*
See *Quick Takes for Teens*, Volume 1, page 40.

### We Are Siblings, Too
*(15 minutes)*
See *Quick Takes for Teens*, Volume 1, page 47.

# Ritual

**2:00 pm** Closing Ritual: Celebrating the Gift of Brothers and Sisters

## Gathering Song
Sing together "All Are Welcome" or "Over My Head."

## Introductory Rite
*Presider:*
> In the name of the Father, Son and Holy Spirit.

*All:*
> Amen.

*Presider:*
> The peace of the Lord be with you.

*All:*
> And also with you.

*Presider:*
> We are all part of a family. Some of us have brothers and sisters, others may have friends or family who are like brothers and sisters. During our time together we have experienced different ways of living and loving these people in our lives. Let us spend some time in prayer recognizing our own giftedness in these relationships.
>
> Let us pray. *(silence)*

God of all gifts, throughout time you have called men and women to live out that special relationship of brothers and sisters. May we take time in our lives to see how you have given each of us special talents to share with our brothers and sisters. Let our actions always praise you as our God. We ask this through Christ our Lord.

*All:*
> Amen.

## Scripture
All stand for the reading of the gospel.

*Reader:*
> The Lord be with you.

*All:*
> And also with you.

*Reader:*
> A reading from the holy gospel according to John.

*All:*
> Glory to you, Lord.

Read John 1:35-42.

*Presider:*
> The gospel of the Lord.

*All:*
> Praise to you, Lord Jesus Christ.

## Psalm
Sing a setting of Psalm 100.

## Reflection
The presider shares a few thoughts on getting along with siblings. See the Introduction, page 5, and additional suggestions in the Advance Preparation Checklist, above.

## Ritual Action
Invite participants to stand. If there are a large number of participants (over 50), break into smaller groups of 15-20. Explain:
- In today's ritual, I'll ask you to complete this sentence:
  — As a brother/sister, the gift I bring to that relationship is...
- If you don't have a sibling, complete this sentence:
  — If I *had* a brother or sister, the gift I would bring to that relationship would be...

*Presider:*
> Good and loving God, we come before you willing to name the gift we bring to the relationship you call family. Our many gifts make up this wonderful yet sometimes challenging situation. Let us offer our special gifts:
>
> As a brother (sister), the gift I bring into my relationship with my sibling(s) is (are)...
>
> *or*
>
> If I *had* a brother (sister), the gift I would bring to that relationship would be...

After the presider completes the sentence, group members take turns doing the same. When all who wish to complete the sentence have done so, continue:

*Presider:*
> Let us name aloud those people in our lives who are brother and sister to us, both our "flesh-and-blood" siblings and those who are as close to us as sisters and brothers.

After *each* name is shared, all respond:
- We thank you, God.

### Concluding Rite
*Presider:*
> Let us pray in the words Christ gave us:

*All:*
> Our Father... Amen.

*Presider:*
> The Lord be with you.

*All:*
> And also with you.

*Presider:*
> God and Father of us all, you called the apostles to follow you and live as brothers in Christ. May we together live as brothers and sisters of light willing to share our lives with each other. And may you bless us, Father, Son and Holy Spirit.

*All:*
> Amen.

*Presider:*
> Let us go forth to love and serve our God and one another.

*All:*
> Thanks be to God.

Invite participants to exchange a Sign of Peace.

### Concluding Song
Sing together "All Are Welcome" or "Over My Head."

**2:25 pm** Evaluation
See the Introduction, page 4.

**2:30 pm** Departure and Team Meeting
See the Introduction, pages 2 and 4.

# RETREAT #4:
## OVERNIGHT MODEL: FAMILY ISSUES

## GETTING READY

### Focus
Retreat #4 blends elements of Retreats #1-3 to take a comprehensive look at how participants interact with their families, including grandparents, parents and siblings. Participants examine the roles they play in their families and look for ways to foster healthier family relationships.

### Core Questions
- How well do we relate with our parents?
- What issues are current in our relationships with our parents?
- How can we improve our relationships with our parents?
- What is sibling rivalry?
- What practical steps can I take to improve my relationships with my brothers and sisters, or with friends with whom I have close, sibling-like relationships?
- How do our families deal with conflict?
- In what ways can careful listening and improved communication reduce conflict?

### Overview
*first day:*
| | |
|---|---|
| 6:00 pm | Team Arrives for Set-Up and Team Meeting |
| 7:00 pm | Participants Arrive |
| 7:15 pm | Welcome: Team Introductions, Rules and Overview of the Retreat |
| 7:30 pm | Session 1: Community Building |
| 8:30 pm | Snack Break and Team Check-In |
| 8:45 pm | Session 2: Family Roots |
| 9:45 pm | Session 3: Pressures and Problems |
| 10:30 pm | Social Time and Team Check-In |
| 11:30 pm | Compline |
| 12:00 am | Bedtime |
| 12:30 am | Lights Out |

*second day:*
| | |
|---|---|
| 8:30 am | Wake Up |
| 9:00 am | Breakfast |
| 9:45 am | Morning Prayer |
| 10:15 am | Session 4: Parents |
| 12:00 pm | Lunch and Team Check-In |
| 1:00 pm | Session 5: Siblings |
| 2:30 pm | Snack Break and Team Check-In |
| 3:00 pm | Session 6: Conflict |
| 4:30 pm | Closing Ritual |
| 4:55 pm | Evaluation |
| 5:00 pm | Departure and Team Meeting |

### Materials
*for the retreat:*
- copies of *Quick Takes for Teens*, Volume 1, 1 per Team Member
- Bibles
- name-tag supplies
- newsprint
- colored felt markers
- masking tape

- three-hole folders, 1 per participant
- colored paper or paper with pre-printed designs
- three-hole punch
- photocopies of Journal Sheets #1 (page 101), #2 (page 102) and #3 (page 103), 1 for each per participant
- photocopies of the Evaluation (page 114), 1 per participant
- CD player
- CDs appropriate for break and reflection times
- index cards
- pens or pencils
- paper
- chairs
- safety pins or masking tape
- food and beverages for breaks and meals

*for the ritual:*
In the Advance Preparation Checklist, below, you will be asked to choose a Closing Ritual for this retreat from Retreats #1, 2 or 3. The materials you will need for that ritual will be found in the materials list for that retreat.

## Advance Preparation Checklist

- [ ] Set the date and reserve the site. Check both school and parish calendars!
- [ ] Read through the Retreat Plan. Decide which activities to include, substitute, adapt, etc.
- [ ] Recruit and train the Retreat Team. See page 1 of the Introduction.
- [ ] Recruit Team Members to give the Witness Talks in Sessions 2 and 4. Besides the basic guidelines given in the Introduction (page 2), suggest to the Team Member giving the Witness Talk in Session 2:
  — In your talk, reflect on 1 Peter 3:9-12.
  — Share about a specific family conflict, how you handled it and how it was resolved.

  Suggest to the Team Member giving the Witness Talk in Session 4:
  — In your talk, reflect on Ephesians 6:1-4.
  — Share an example of your own experiences—both good and bad—communicating with your parents.
- [ ] Create Retreat Journals for each participant:
  — Photocopy Journal Sheets #1, #2, and #3.
  — Alternate the Journal Sheets with sheets of blank paper.
  — Three-hole punch all sheets and bind them in three-hole folders.
  — For visual interest, use colorful paper or paper with pre-printed designs, available at office supply stores.
- [ ] Choose the ritual you think is most appropriate from Retreat 1 (page 12, on Conflict), Retreat 2 (page 18, on Parents) or Retreat 3 (page 24, on Siblings). Decide who will preside at the Closing Ritual. Ask the presider to prepare the Reflection to be given in the ritual. Specific suggestions for these Reflections are given in the corresponding Advance Preparation Checklist in each of the three retreats.
- [ ] Arrange for food and beverages.
- [ ] Arrange for transportation, as necessary.
- [ ] Get permission slips, as necessary.
- [ ] Photocopy necessary materials, for example, Journal Sheets and Evaluations.
- [ ] Arrange for each participant to bring several photographs of their parents, grandparents or other older relatives.
- [ ] Copy onto poster board the quotes found in "Quote Parents Unquote," *Quick Takes for Teens*, Volume 1, page 37. You won't be using the activity, but the quotes offer food for thought throughout the retreat. Tape these to the walls of the meeting room.
- [ ] Collect and pack materials.
- [ ] Envision the environment and prepare necessary materials. See the Introduction, page 2.
- [ ] Pre-assign participants to small groups. Assign a Team Member to facilitate each group. Determine locations for small-group discussions.

## RETREAT PLAN

*first day:*

**6:00 pm**   Team Arrives for Set-Up and Team Meeting
See the Introduction, page 2.

**7:00 pm** Participants Arrive

**Name Tags**
See the Introduction, page 3.

**7:15 pm** Welcome
See the Introduction, pages 3-4.

**Team Introductions**
(5 minutes)

**Rules and Overview of the Day**
(5 minutes)

**Distribution of Journals**
(5 minutes)
Distribute pens or pencils and the Retreat Journals prepared before the retreat. Explain:
- Throughout the retreat, feel free to use the blank pages in your Retreat Journal to record your feelings, thoughts, ideas and reaction.
- One of the Journal Sheets—#2—will be used in an activity we will do together.
- The remaining two Journal Sheets—#1 and #3—are yours to use as you wish.
- Please put your name on the front of your folder, to help you keep track of it.

If time allows, you could invite participants to list on one of the blank pages of their Retreat Journals two or three hopes they have for the retreat. Ask volunteers to share what they have written.

**7:30 pm** Session 1: Community Building
We suggest the following icebreakers. Add your favorites or choose others from *Quick Takes for Teens*, Volume 1, pages 6-7.

**Introductions**
(15 minutes)
See *Quick Takes for Teens Volume 1*, page 7.

**My Ideal**
(15 minutes)
See *Quick Takes for Teens Volume 1*, page 6.

**8:30 pm** Snack Break and Team Check-In
See the Introduction, page 2.

**8:45 pm** Session 2: Family Roots

**Family Roles**
(30 minutes)
See *Quick Takes for Teens*, Volume 1, page 26.

**The Characters**
(30 minutes)
See *Quick Takes for Teens*, Volume 1, page 27.

Divide participants into smaller groups of 7-9 members each for this activity.

**9:45 pm** Session 3: Pressures and Problems

**Witness Talk**
(10 minutes)
See the Introduction, page 3, and the Advance Preparation Checklist, above.

Regather the large group. Introduce the Team Member giving the Witness Talk.

**A Bag of Pressure**
(35 minutes)
See *Quick Takes for Teens*, Volume 1, page 13.

Introduce this activity by inviting participants to return to the small groups of the previous session, then explaining that all members will now have an opportunity to explore how conflict surfaces in their own families. Distribute index cards to all participants. Make sure they all also have pens or pencils.

**10:30 pm** Social Time and Team Check-In
See the Introduction, page 2.

**11:30 pm** Compline
See the Introduction, pages 6-7.

**12:00 pm** Bedtime

**12:30 pm** Lights Out

*second day:*
**8:30 am** Wake Up

**9:00 am** Breakfast

**9:45 am** Morning Prayer
See the Introduction, pages 6-7.

### Making Room
See *Quick Takes for Teens*, Volume 1, page 41.

Conclude the discussion with petitions offered for families. After each prayer, the group responds:
- We pray to the Lord.

**10:15 am** Session 4: Parents

### Family Stories
*(15 minutes)*
Invite participants to share stories about their grandparents. After all who wish to share a story have done so, discuss:
- What do you imagine life was like for our grandparents when *they* were teenagers? How might their teenage years have been similar to ours? different?

### Journal Reflection
*(15 minutes)*
Distribute pens or pencils and copies of Journal #2. Invite group members to complete their journal sheets. As they do so, they will get more in touch with their thoughts and feelings about their grandparents.

After 10 minutes of journal reflection, divide participants into smaller groups of 7-9 members each. Ask group members to share their reflections with each other.

### Inheritance
*(15 minutes)*
See *Quick Takes for Teens*, Volume 1, page 31.

Regather the large group for this activity. In particular, focus on the questions after the second bullet, which stress how families "hand down" ways of relating from generation to generation.

### Stretch Break
*(5 minutes)*

### Communicating with Parents
*(20 minutes)*
See *Quick Takes for Teens*, Volume 1, page 12.

### Witness Talk
*(10 minutes)*
See Introduction, page 2, and the Advance Preparation Checklist, above.

### Freeze Frames
*(25 minutes)*
See *Quick Takes for Teens*, Volume 1, page 30.

As written in *Quick Takes*, this activity invites group members to pose scenes that reflect dynamics in their families. As you use the activity here, however, ask group members to pose a scene that specifically shows their relationship *with their parents*. If other family members appear in the scenes, that's fine, but be certain that they also echo the relationship of teens *with parents*. Model the activity for group members first, and let them know that they may pose any issue they currently have with their parents. Some of these issues may be painful; be prepared to identify and facilitate their expression.

Conclude the activity by discussing:
- What parent/teen issues surfaced in this activity?
- How many of these are current issues for others of us in the group?
- What similarities to these scenes do you see in your own family? What differences?
- How do you deal with these issues with *your* parents?

**12:00 pm** Lunch and Team Check-In
See the Introduction, page 2.

**1:00 pm** Session 5: Siblings

### Sibling Songs
*(20 minutes)*
See *Quick Takes for Teens,* Volume 1, page 45.

### Compatible?
*(20 minutes)*
See *Quick Takes for Teens,* Volume 1, page 43.

The instructions for this activity suggest that you prepare and conduct a sibling survey *prior* to the meeting. Instead, *begin* the activity by informally conducting the survey, keeping track of the results on newsprint. Note that there are two parts to the survey, first, some general questions, and second, five items that group members rate on a scale of 1 (low) to 10 (high).

After the survey, discuss the three questions found at the end of the activity.

### Real Dialogue
*(25 minutes)*
See *Quick Takes for Teens,* Volume 1, page 42.

### Parable Rewrite
*(25 minutes)*
See *Quick Takes for Teens,* Volume 1, page 43.

**2:30 pm** Snack Break and Team Check-In
See the Introduction, page 2.

**3:00 pm** Session 6: Conflict

### Who Gets a Chair?
*(30 minutes)*
See *Quick Takes for Teens,* Volume 1, page 9.

At the conclusion of "Who Gets a Chair?" invite participants to brainstorm different types of conflict. Record their suggestions on newsprint. Examples could include specific issues of conflict within families, friendships, the world, religions, political structures, nature, etc.

After compiling the list, discuss:
- How does conflict start?
- What feelings add to conflict? *(fear, loss, competition, jealousy, etc.)*
- What words describe the end of conflict? *(peace, serenity, joy, love, etc.)*

### Yes/No
*(25 minutes)*
Share the following, in these or your own words:
- In this session, we explore ways in which we communicate with each other. Some ways are helpful; others are not.
- Let's see if we can learn new ways of communicating by sharing what is inside of us, rather than attacking what we imagine is in the other person.

Offer these directions to group members:
- Find a partner. Sit face to face with your partner.
- With your partner, decide which of you will be *the parent* and which will be *the teenager*.

- Now, for the next 15 second, *the parent* will say the word *no* repeatedly, and only the word *no*. Meanwhile, *the teenager* will say the word *yes* repeatedly, but only the word *yes*.
- Are you ready? On your mark, get set, *go!*

After 15 seconds, stop participants and switch the scenario as suggested below. There are five more rounds, each of which lasts 15 seconds:
- Round 2: *The parent* continues to say *no*. *The teenager* continues to say *yes*. *The parent*, however, *stands up*.
- Round 3: *The parent* continues to say *no*. *The teenager* continue to say *yes*. This time, however, *the parent sits down* and *the teenager stands up*. Remind partners of their parent and teenager roles.
- Round 4: *The parent* remains seated. *The teenager* remains standing. This time, *the parent* says *yes* and *the teenager* says *no*.
- Round 5: Both *the parent* and *the teenager stand up*. *The parent* continues to say *yes* and *the teenager* continues to say *no*. Once again remind partners of their parent and teenager roles.
- Round 6: Both *the parent* and *the teenager* remain *standing* and both say *yes*.

Invite participants to be seated and discuss:
- As you participated, what, in *your* mind, were you arguing about?
- As the rounds progressed, what did you notice about the way you felt?
- What were you wanting to say that you couldn't?
- How did you feel being at different levels? the same level?
- What does this activity illustrate about how we interact with our parents?
- In what way does "being on the same level" with our parents or other family members help communication?

**Stretch Break**
*(5 minutes)*
Give group members a brief break while you prepare for the next activity.

**Practice!**
*(30 minutes)*
See *Quick Takes for Teens*, Volume 1, page 14.

Introduce this activity by saying:
- Good listening is critical for both preventing and resolving conflict.
- Let's see what we learn about these important skills in this activity.

**4:30 pm**   Closing Ritual

**4:55 pm**   Evaluation
See the Introduction, page 4.

**5:00 pm**   Departure and Team Meeting
See the Introduction, pages 2 and 4.

# CHAPTER 2

## RETREAT #5:
### STRESS AND DEPRESSION

## GETTING READY

### Focus
Retreat #5 invites participants to explore their personal struggles with stress and depression. Not only will they share their experiences, but also discover ways to cope, including finding strength and comfort in scripture and each other.

### Core Questions
- What is stress? What is depression? What contributes to these in our lives?
- How do we — in healthy and unhealthy ways — cope with stress and depression?
- What help for overcoming stress and depression can we find in scripture?
- How can we help one another deal with stress and depression?

### Overview
| | |
|---|---|
| 8:00 am | Team Arrives for Set-Up and Team Meeting |
| 9:00 am | Participants Arrive |
| 9:15 am | Welcome: Team Introductions, Rules and Overview of the Day |
| 9:30 am | Session 1: Community Building |
| 10:15 am | Snack Break and Team Check-In |
| 10:30 am | Session 2: Stressed Out! |
| 11:30 am | Lunch and Team Check-In |
| 12:15 pm | Session 3: Depression |
| 1:15 pm | Session 4: Let's *Un*stress! |
| 2:00 pm | Closing Ritual: Comfort in Jesus' Presence |
| 2:25 pm | Evaluation |
| 2:30 pm | Departure and Team Meeting |

### Materials
*for the retreat:*
- copies of *Quick Takes for Teens*, Volume 2, 1 per Team Leader
- Bibles
- name-tag supplies
- photocopies of Journal #5 (page 104), 1 per participant
- photocopies of the Evaluation (page 114), 1 per participant
- pens or pencils
- index cards
- People Bingo cards (See the Advance Preparation Checklist, below.)
- CD player
- CDs appropriate for break and reflection times
- newsprint
- masking tape
- colored felt markers
- food and beverages for breaks and lunch

*for the ritual:*
- printed or recorded music:
  — "Be Still and Know That I Am God" by John Bell (Iona Community, distributed in the U.S. by GIA) or "Tuhan Dengar Doa Kami" by Steve Manibusan (OCP)
  — "The Breath of God" by Steven Petrunak (GIA) or "Free Fall" by Patrick Loomas (OCP)
  — a musical setting of Psalm 16 that is familiar to your community

— "Behold I Make All Things New" by John Bell (Iona Community, distributed in the U.S. by GIA) or "Talkin' 'Bout" by Tom Booth (OCP)

## Advance Preparation Checklist

☐ Set the date and reserve the site. Check both school and parish calendars!
☐ Read through the Retreat Plan. Decide which activities to include, substitute, adapt, etc.
☐ Recruit and train the Retreat Team. See the Introduction, page 1.
☐ Decide who will preside at the Closing Ritual. Ask the presider to prepare the Reflection to be given in the ritual. In the Reflection, the presider shares thoughts on stress and depression. The following questions also may help in preparation:
  — When in your life have your struggled with stress and/or depression?
  — What part has God played in your struggle with these emotions?
  — What scripture story (or stories) help you cope with stress and/or depression?
  — What images of God and Jesus support you in times of stress and low feelings?

As a part of the Reflection, the presider may wish to have the assembly reflect on any one of these same questions, either silently or in groups of no more than three members each.

☐ Recruit a Team Member to give the Witness Talk in Session 2. Besides the basic guidelines given in the Introduction (page 2), suggest to the Team Member:
  — In your talk, reflect on Philippians 4:4-9.
  — Share a personal experience of stress, for example, "the worst week of my life" or "how stress destroyed our family's communication."
☐ Prepare the cards for People Bingo, the recommended icebreaker. For instructions, see "People Bingo," *Quick Takes for Teens*, Volume 2, page 6.
☐ Arrange for food and beverages.
☐ Arrange for transportation, as necessary.
☐ Get permission slips, as necessary.
☐ Photocopy necessary materials, for example, Journal Sheets and Evaluations.
☐ Collect and pack materials.
☐ Envision the environment and prepare necessary materials. See the Introduction, page 2.
☐ Pre-assign participants to small groups. Assign a Team Member to facilitate each group. Determine locations for small-group discussions.

## RETREAT PLAN

**8:00 am** Team Arrives for Set-Up and Team Meeting
See the Introduction, page 2.

**9:00 am** Participants Arrive

**Name Tags**
See the Introduction, page 3.

**9:15 am** Welcome
See the Introduction, pages 3-4.

**Team Introductions**
*(5 minutes)*

**Rules**
*(5 minutes)*

**Overview of the Day**
*(5 minutes)*

**9:30 am** Session 1: Community Building
We suggest the following icebreaker. Add your favorites or choose others from *Quick Takes for Teens*, Volume 2, pages 6-7.

**People Bingo**
*(25 minutes)*
See *Quick Takes for Teens*, Volume 2, page 6.

**10:15 am** Snack Break and Team Check-In
See the Introduction, page 2.

**10:30 am** Session 2: Stressed Out!

### The Worst Day of My Life
*(20 minutes)*
See *Quick Takes for Teens*, Volume 2, page 22.

### Stress Evaluation
*(15 minutes)*
See *Quick Takes for Teens*, Volume 2, page 19.

### Stress Response
*(15 minutes)*
See *Quick Takes for Teens*, Volume 2, page 20.

Refocus the group's attention and introduce the Witness Talk Team member.

### Witness Talk
*(10 minutes)*
See the Introduction, page 2, and the Advance Preparation Checklist, above.

**11:30 am** Lunch and Team Meeting
See the Introduction, page 2.

**12:15 pm** Session 3: Depression

### Understanding Depression
*(15 minutes)*
See *Quick Takes for Teens*, Volume 2, page 19.

### In Other Words
*(10 minutes)*
See *Quick Takes for Teens*, Volume 2, page 22.

### Journal Reflection
*(15 minutes)*
Distribute pens or pencils, Bibles and photocopies of Journal #5. Invite participants to work individually to complete the sheet.

After about 10 minutes, regather and invite volunteers to share their insights with the group.

### Human Gumby®
*(15 minutes)*
See *Quick Takes for Teens*, Volume 2, page 23.

### Stretch Break
*(5 minutes)*
Give group members a brief break while you prepare for the next session.

**1:15 pm** Session 4: Let's *Un*stress!

### Coping
*(25 minutes)*
See *Quick Takes for Teens*, Volume 2, page 18.

### The Bigger Picture
*(20 minutes)*
See *Quick Takes for Teens*, Volume 2, page 21.

## Ritual

**2:00 pm** Closing Ritual: Comfort in Jesus' Presence

### Gathering Song
Sing together "Be Still and Know That I Am God" or "Tuhan Dengar Doa Kami."

### Introductory Rite
*Presider:*
In the name of the Father, Son and Holy Spirit.

*All:*
    Amen.

*Presider:*
    The Lord be with you.

*All:*
    And also with you.

*Presider:*
    As we gather, we take time to reflect on those times when we feel stressed out or low in spirit. Let us turn to God and to one another for support during this time together, recognizing that God is present inside each of us, and that, as we turn to one another during this ritual, we are ministers of God's presence to each other.

**Opening Prayer**

*Presider:*
    Let us pray. *(silence)*

    Protective God, sometimes we feel alone and afraid inside. You call us to take our loneliness and fear to you. Give us the light we need when we feel surrounded by the dark. Help us make good choices. Lead us to ask for your help, through Christ our Lord,

*All:*
    Amen.

(Prayer adapted from Jamie Hinde in *God of My Heart*, Connie Wlaschin Ruhlman, compiler and editor, Living the Good News, Denver: 1998, page 114.)

**Scripture**

*Presider:*
    A reading from Paul's letter to the Philippians.

Read aloud Philippians 4:4-9.

*Presider:*
    The word of the Lord.

*All:*
    Thanks be to God.

**Psalm**
Sing a setting of Psalm 16.

**Reflection**
The presider shares a few thoughts on stress and depression. See Introduction, page 5, and the Advance Preparation Checklist, above.

**Ritual Action**
Play live or recorded instrumental music in the background, either "The Breath of God" or "Free Fall."

Invite participants to form pairs. Ask pairs to spread out around the meeting space, sitting together on chairs or on the floor, with one partner seated behind the other. The partner seated *behind* is Partner 1, who will be present for Partner 2 in the following meditation. Partner 1 puts his or her hands on the shoulders, back or neck of Partner 2. Partner 1 says nothing, but silently communicates to Partner 2, through touch, that he or she is there to support and comfort.

*Presider:*
    If you are Partner 2, I invite you now silently to turn to God with your stress and depression. Let God know what you feel, what you fear, what you hope, what you desire.

    If you are Partner 1, be the loving hands of God for your partner; offer your partner companionship and support through your quiet touch.

Lead participants through the meditation in "Unstress" (*Quick Takes for Teens*, Volume 2, page 18).

Allow a minute of silence after the meditation, then ask partners to switch (Partner 1 becomes Partner 2, Partner 2 becomes Partner 1). Repeat the activity.

Allow another minute of silence after repeating the meditation, then invite participants to share what they felt and experienced.

*Presider:*
> Having shared our feelings, let us stand together as one community.

Form a circle and join hands. Continue with the Concluding Rite.

**Concluding Rite**

*Presider:*
> Let us pray in the words Christ gave us:

*All:*
> Our Father... Amen.

*Presider:*
> Let us pray:
>
> God of Guidance, you gave us your only Son, Jesus, as a sign of your abundant love for us. Sometimes, though, we lose faith—we doubt that you even care about us. When it seems like no one is on our side, that everyone is against us, please help us to be strong and to experience the resurrection of your Son, Jesus. Let us realize that we are not alone, and that you are truly here for us, to lead and support us.

> We ask this through Christ our Lord,

*All:*
> Amen.

(Prayer adapted from Letitia Halverson in *God of My Heart*, Connie Wlaschin Ruhlman, compiler and editor, Living the Good News, Denver: 1998, page 60.)

*Presider:*
> The Lord be with you.

*All:*
> And also with you.

*Presider:*
> May almighty God bless us, Father, Son and Holy Spirit.

*All:*
> Amen.

*Presider:*
> Let us go forth to love and serve our God and one another.

*All:*
> Thanks be to God.

Invite participants to exchange a Sign of Peace.

**Concluding Song**

Sing together "Behold I Make All Things New" or "Talkin' 'Bout."

**2:25 pm** Evaluation
See the Introduction, page 4.

**2:30 pm** Departure and Team Meeting
See the Introduction, pages 2 and 4.

# TOUGH EMOTIONS RETREATS

## RETREAT #6:
### ANGER AND HATRED

## GETTING READY

### Focus
Retreat #6 explores two potent emotions—anger and hatred. Participants examine the consequences of anger and hatred, then learn healthy ways to cope with them.

### Core Questions
- Why do we feel angry? Why do we hate?
- How can we express our anger in healthy, constructive ways?
- What are the roots of hatred?
- How can hatred be overcome with love?
- What does God have to say to us about anger and hatred?

### Overview
| | |
|---|---|
| 8:00 am | Team Arrives for Set-Up and Team Meeting |
| 9:00 am | Participants Arrive |
| 9:15 am | Welcome: Team Introductions, Rules and Overview of the Day |
| 9:30 am | Session 1: Community Building |
| 10:15 am | Snack Break and Team Check-In |
| 10:30 am | Session 2: Exploring Anger |
| 11:30 am | Lunch Break and Team Check-In |
| 12:15 pm | Session 3: Exploring Hatred |
| 1:15 pm | Session 4: Healthier Alternatives |
| 2:00 pm | Closing Ritual: From Anger to Peace, From Hatred to Love |
| 2:25 pm | Evaluation |
| 2:30 pm | Departure and Team Meeting |

### Materials
*for the retreat:*
- copies of *Quick Takes for Teens*, Volume 2, 1 per Team Leader
- Bibles
- name-tag supplies
- photocopies of Journal #6 (page 105), 1 per participant
- photocopies of the Evaluation (page 114), 1 per participant
- art supplies (paper and crayons, modeling clay, etc.)
- construction toys (Tinker Toys®, Legos®, etc.)
- pens or pencils
- index cards
- discarded watch (or other item of value)
- block of wood
- hammer
- pipe cleaners
- CD player
- CDs appropriate for break and reflection times
- newsprint
- masking tape
- colored felt markers
- food and beverages for breaks and lunch

*for the ritual:*
- copies of songs
  — "Standin' in the Need of Prayer" (African-American spiritual) or "Come to Us, Spirit of Jesus" by Mark Friedman (OCP)
  — a musical setting of Psalm 55 that is familiar to your community

— "Joyfully Singing" by Balhoff, Daigle and Ducote (Damean Music, distributed in the U.S. by GIA) or "Our God Reigns" by Leonard E. Smith, Jr. (New Jerusalem Music, as recorded by Tom Booth on "Tom Booth," OCP)

## Advance Preparation Checklist

- ☐ Set the date and reserve the site. Check both school and parish calendars!
- ☐ Read through the Retreat Plan. Decide which activities to include, substitute, adapt, etc.
- ☐ Recruit and train the Retreat Team. See the Introduction, page 1.
- ☐ Decide who will preside at the Closing Ritual. Ask the presider to prepare the Reflection to be given in the ritual. In the Reflection, the presider shares thoughts on anger and/or hatred. The following questions may help in preparation:
  — When in your life have you felt like anger was a problem for you? for someone you cared about?
  — How can anger be expressed in *healthy* ways? *unhealthy* ways?
  — What is the difference between anger and hatred?
  — What damage have you seen done by hatred?
  — Where is hatred a problem in your own life?
  — How do we replace hatred with love?
  
  As a part of the Reflection, the presider may wish to have the assembly reflect on any one of these same questions, either silently or in groups of no more than three members each.
- ☐ Recruit a Team Member to give the Witness Talk in Session 3. Beside the basic guidelines given in the Introduction (page 2), suggest to the Team Member:
  — In your talk, reflect on Proverbs 10:12.
  — Share a personal experience of hatred, for example, a time when hatred caused pain to you or someone you loved, and how you overcame the hatred.
- ☐ Recruit a guest speaker to join you for a presentation on hate crimes as part of the activity "What Hath Anger Wrought?" in Session 3. For suggestions, see the instructions for the activity in *Quick Takes for Teens*, Volume 2, page 12.
- ☐ Arrange for food and beverages.
- ☐ Arrange for transportation, as necessary.
- ☐ Get permission slips, as necessary.
- ☐ Photocopy necessary materials, for example, Journal Sheets and Evaluations.
- ☐ Collect and pack materials.
- ☐ Envision the environment and prepare necessary materials. See the Introduction, page 2.
- ☐ Pre-assign participants to small groups. Assign a Team Member to facilitate each group. Determine locations for small-group discussions.

## RETREAT PLAN

**8:00 am** Team Arrives for Set-Up and Team Meeting
See the Introduction, page 2.

**9:00 am** Participants Arrive

**Name Tags**
See the Introduction, page 3.

**9:15 am** Welcome
See the Introduction, pages 3-4.

**Team Introductions**
*(5 minutes)*

**Rules**
*(5 minutes)*

**Overview of the Day**
*(5 minutes)*

**9:30 am** Session 1: Community Building
We suggest the following icebreaker. Add your favorites or choose others from *Quick Takes for Teens*, Volume 2, pages 6-7.

**Picture Your Week**
*(20 minutes)*
See *Quick Takes for Teens*, Volume 2, page 7.

**10:15 am** Snack Break and Team Check-In
See the Introduction, page 2.

**10:30 am** Session 2: Exploring Anger

**Smash It!**
*(10 minutes)*
See *Quick Takes for Teens*, Volume 2, page 8.

**Anger Symbols**
*(15 minutes)*
See *Quick Takes for Teens*, Volume 2, page 12.

**Examining Anger**
*(20 minutes)*
See *Quick Takes for Teens*, Volume 2, page 9.

**Great Quotes, Part I**
*(15 minutes)*
See *Quick Takes for Teens*, Volume 2, page 13.

**11:30 am** Lunch and Team Check-In
See the Introduction, page 2.

**12:15 pm** Session 3: Exploring Hatred

**Hate Tour**
*(15 minutes)*
See *Quick Takes for Teens*, Volume 2, page 13.

**What Hath Anger Wrought?**
*(30 minutes)*
See *Quick Takes for Teens*, Volume 2, page 12.

Refocus the group's attention and introduce the Witness Talk Team member.

**Witness Talk**
*(10 minutes)*
See the Introduction, page 2, and the Advance Preparation Checklist.

**Stretch Break**
*(5 minutes)*
Give group members a brief break while you prepare for the next session.

**1:15 pm** Session 4: Healthier Alternatives

**Love Tour**
*(15 minutes)*
See *Quick Takes for Teens*, Volume 2, page 14.

**Healthy Anger**
*(20 minutes)*
See *Quick Takes for Teens*, Volume 2, page 10.

**Journal Reflection**
*(10 minutes)*
Distribute pens or pencils, Bibles and photocopies of Journal #6. Invite participants to work individually to complete the sheet.

After about 5 minutes, regather and invite volunteers to share their insights with the group.

# Ritual

**2:00 pm** Closing Ritual: From Anger to Peace, from Hatred to Love

## Gathering Song
Sing together "Standin' in the Need of Prayer" or "Come to Us, Spirit of Jesus."

## Introductory Rite
*Presider:*
   In the name of the Father, Son and Holy Spirit.

*All:*
   Amen.

*Presider:*
   The Lord be with you.

*All:*
   And also with you.

*Presider:*
   Recognizing ourselves as people who are human, we ask God for help — when angry, to express that anger in healthy ways; when hateful, to replace the hatred with God's endless love.

## Opening Prayer
*Presider:*
   Let us pray. *(silence)*

   God of Power, it's tough to know how to put up with people when they anger us. We want to control our anger, and to learn to judge people fairly. We appreciate your understanding and kindness in helping us deal with this. Help us not to let anger control our lives. Help us to use it's power wisely, and to find ways to let it be a positive force in our lives, through Christ our Lord.

*All:*
   Amen.

(Prayer adapted from Paul Gilg in *God of My Heart*, Connie Wlaschin Ruhlman, compiler and editor, Living the Good News, Denver: 1998, page 113.)

## Scripture
*Presider:*
   A reading from the letter to the Ephesians.

Read aloud Ephesians 4:26-32.

*Presider:*
   The word of the Lord.

*All:*
   Thanks be to God.

## Psalm
Sing a setting of Psalm 55.

## Reflection
The presider shares a few thoughts on anger and hatred. See the Introduction, page 5, and the Advance Preparation Checklist, above.

## Ritual Action
Lead participants through the "Silent Meditation," *Quick Takes for Teens*, Volume 2, page 11.

## Concluding Rite
*Presider:*
   Let us pray in the words Christ gave us:

*All:*
   Our Father... Amen.

*Presider:*
Let us pray. *(silence)*

God of Love, you gave us your only Son, Jesus, as a sign of your abundant love for us. Sometimes, though, we lose our confidence in that great gift; we feel threatened, frightened, small, alone, easily believing that others oppose us. Remind us at these times that we are truly loved, and that in you we find meaning, peace and hope.

Give us confidence to face and express our anger in ways that lead to healing, not hurt. Help us to release our hatred, and discover in you the love we need to turn to others in understanding and love.

We ask this through Christ our Lord,

*All:*
Amen.

*Presider:*
The Lord be with you.

*All:*
And also with you.

*Presider:*
May almighty God bless us, Father, Son and Holy Spirit.

*All:*
Amen.

*Presider:*
Let us go forth to love and serve our God and one another.

*All:*
Thanks be to God.

Invite participants to exchange a Sign of Peace.

**Concluding Song**
Sing together "Joyfully Singing" or "Our God Reigns."

**2:25 pm**   Evaluation
See the Introduction, page 4.

**2:30 pm**   Departure and Team Meeting
See the Introduction, pages 2 and 4.

# RETREAT #7:
## FACING INSECURITY AND BUILDING SELF-ESTEEM

## GETTING READY

### Focus
Retreat #7 looks at the causes and results of insecurity and low self-esteem. Participants are invited to take steps toward self-understanding and acceptance, and to offer one another affirmation.

### Core Questions
- What do we fear? What is the root of our fear and insecurity?
- How do we cope with falling, failing and feeling rejected?
- What is healthy self-esteem? self-confidence? How do these develop? What steps can we take to strengthen self-confidence and self-esteem?
- What's the relationship of faith to insecurity and self-confidence?

### Overview
| | |
|---|---|
| 8:00 am | Team Arrives for Set-Up and Team Meeting |
| 9:00 am | Participants Arrive |
| 9:15 am | Welcome: Team Introductions, Rules and Overview of the Day |
| 9:30 am | Session 1: Community Building |
| 10:15 am | Snack Break and Team Check-In |
| 10:30 am | Session 2: Understanding Our Emotions |
| 11:30 am | Lunch and Team Check-In |
| 12:15 pm | Session 3: Self-Esteem |
| 1:15 pm | Session 4: Affirmation |
| 2:00 pm | Closing Ritual: Found by God |
| 2:25 pm | Evaluation |
| 2:30 pm | Departure and Team Meeting |

### Materials
*for the retreat:*
- copies of *Quick Takes for Teens*, Volume 2, 1 per Team Leader
- Bibles
- name-tag supplies
- photocopies of Journal #7 (page 106), 1 per participant
- photocopies of the Evaluation (page 114), 1 per participant
- small blocks of wood
- pens or pencils
- index cards
- hat or basket
- CD player
- CDs appropriate for break and reflection times
- newsprint
- masking tape
- colored felt markers
- food and beverages for breaks and lunch

*for the ritual:*
- recorded or printed music:
  — "You Are Mine" by David Haas (GIA) or "Blessed Are They" by Steve Agrisano (OCP)
  — a musical setting of Psalm 51 that is familiar to your community
  — "All Are Welcome" by Marty Haugen (GIA) or "Working for the Lord" by Fr. Richard Ho Lung, M.O.P. (OCP)

### Advance Preparation Checklist
- ☐ Set the date and reserve the site. Check both school and parish calendars!

- ☐ Read through the Retreat Plan. Decide which activities to include, substitute, adapt, etc.
- ☐ Recruit and train the Retreat Team. See the Introduction, page 1.
- ☐ Decide who will preside at the Closing Ritual. Ask the presider to prepare the Reflection to be given in the ritual. In the Reflection, the presider shares thoughts on fear, insecurity, self-esteem and self-confidence. The following questions may help in preparation:
  — When have you felt lost, alone and insecure?
  — At such times of low self-esteem, who in your own life has welcomed and affirmed you?
  — What part does God play in the development of healthy self-esteem?
  — What challenges you from reaching out to those who feel like "outsiders"?

  As a part of the Reflection, the presider may wish to have the assembly reflect on any one of these same questions, either silently or in groups of no more than three members each.
- ☐ Recruit a Team Member to give the Witness Talk in Session 2. Beside the basic guidelines given in the Introduction (page 2), suggest to the Team Member:
  — In your talk, reflect on Romans 8:31-39.
  — Share a personal experience of fear and insecurity, and what gave you the courage the believe in yourself.
- ☐ Prepare the roleplay cards for the activity "Self-Esteem Roleplay" in Session 3. For directions, see *Quick Takes for Teens*, Volume 2, page 46.
- ☐ Arrange for food and beverages.
- ☐ Arrange for transportation, as necessary.
- ☐ Get permission slips, as necessary.
- ☐ Photocopy necessary materials, for example, Journal Sheets and Evaluations.
- ☐ Collect and pack materials.
- ☐ Envision the environment and prepare necessary materials. See the Introduction, page 2.
- ☐ Pre-assign participants to small groups. Assign a Team Member to facilitate each group. Determine locations for small-group discussions.

## RETREAT PLAN

**8:00 am** Team Arrives for Set-Up and Team Meeting
See the Introduction, page 2.

**9:00 am** Participants Arrive

**Name Tags**
See the Introduction, page 3.

**9:15 am** Welcome
See the Introduction, pages 3-4.

**Team Introductions**
*(5 minutes)*

**Rules**
*(5 minutes)*

**Overview of the Day**
*(5 minutes)*

**9:30 am** Session 1: Community Building
We suggest the following icebreaker. Add your favorites or choose others from *Quick Takes for Teens*, Volume 2, pages 6-7.

**Children's Games**
*(20 minutes)*
See *Quick Takes for Teens*, Volume 2, page 7.

**The Insecurity Song**
*(15 minutes)*
See *Quick Takes for Teens*, Volume 2, page 43.

**10:15 am** Snack Break and Team Check-In
See the Introduction, page 2.

**10:30 am** Session 2: Understanding Our Emotions

**Building Blocks**
*(25 minutes)*
See *Quick Takes for Teens*, Volume 2, page 42.

### Emotion Walk
*(10 minutes)*
Invite group members to stand in a large circle. Recruit a volunteer to stand in the middle of the circle. Explain:
- As a group, start walking clockwise around the circle.
- Once we start walking, I'll call out a feeling. When I've named the feeling, start walking *as if you were feeling that feeling*. Let your movements, posture and facial expressions reflect the feeling I've named.
- After a few seconds, I'll call out another feeling. Change your walk to reflect that new feeling.

Here are several emotions to name; add others if you wish, or invite volunteers to call out other emotions for group members to mirror. *Be certain to end with* insecurity:
- anger
- love
- loneliness
- happiness
- hate
- fear
- insecurity

### Emotion Talk
*(15 minutes)*
See *Quick Takes for Teens*, Volume 2, page 39.

Refocus the group's attention and introduce the Witness Talk Team member.

### Witness Talk
*(10 minutes)*
See the Introduction, page 2, and the Advance Preparation Checklist, above.

**11:30 am** Lunch and Team Meeting
See the Introduction, page 2.

**12:15 pm** Session 3: Self-Esteem

### Self-Esteem Killers
*(10 minutes)*
See *Quick Takes for Teens*, Volume 2, page 47.

### Creative Movement
*(10 minutes)*
See *Quick Takes for Teens*, Volume 2, page 47.

### Self-Esteem Roleplay
*(25 minutes)*
See *Quick Takes for Teens*, Volume 2, page 46.

### Let's Pretend, Part I
*(10 minutes)*
See *Quick Takes for Teens*, Volume 2, page 42.

### Stretch Break
*(5 minutes)*
Give group members a brief break while you prepare for the next session.

**1:15 pm** Session 4: Affirmation

### Secure
*(15 minutes)*
See *Quick Takes for Teens*, Volume 2, page 39.

### Let's Pretend, Part II
*(15 minutes)*
See *Quick Takes for Teens*, Volume 2, page 43.

### Journal Reflection
*(15 minutes)*
Distribute pens or pencils, envelopes, stamps and photocopies of Journal #7. Invite participants to work individually to complete the sheet.

After about 10 minutes, regather and invite volunteers to share their letters with the group. After sharing, ask participants to seal their letters and stamp their envelopes. Collect these to mail to participants in the next day or two.

# Ritual

**2:00 pm**  Closing Ritual: Found by God

## Gathering Song
Sing together "You Are Mine" or "Blessed Are They."

## Introductory Rite

*Presider:*
> In the name of the Father, Son and Holy Spirit.

*All:*
> Amen.

*Presider:*
> The Lord be with you.

*All:*
> And also with you.

*Presider:*
> As we come to this prayer, we bring our fears and our lack of confidence—and the knowledge that God is present and eager to help us. May this prayer open our hearts and minds to the love God has for us.
>
> Let us pray. *(silence)*
>
> God of all strength and fortitude, you are present to our every need and seek us out when we stray from your path. May we open our hearts and minds to your forgiveness, and may we recognize that we are called to live as children of light and love. We praise you as the God who lives forever and ever.

*All:*
> Amen.

## Scripture
All stand for the reading of the gospel.

*Presider:*
> The Lord be with you.

*All:*
> And also with you.

*Presider:*
> A reading from the holy gospel according to...

*All:*
> Glory to you, Lord.

Read aloud Luke 15:4-7.

*Presider:*
> The gospel of the Lord.

*All:*
> Praise to you, Lord Jesus Christ.

## Psalm
Sing a setting of Psalm 51.

## Reflection
The presider shares a few thoughts on insecurity and self-esteem. See the Introduction, page 5, and the Advance Preparation Checklist, above.

## Ritual Action

*Presider:*
> When the church welcomes new members into the journey of the catechumenate (coming into the Catholic faith), there is a ritual where we mark one another with the sign of the cross. I invite you to turn one another and to welcome each other into the love of God by marking one another's foreheads with the Sign of the Cross, thus remembering that God is with us.

...e of Signing of the Senses (para. 56 of Rites of Christian ...tiation of Adults). Adapt as necessary for your group and the setting.

**Litany of Self-Esteem**

*Presider:*
Knowing that God is with us, let us lift up to God something good that is going on in our lives:

For those in our church who search for those who feel alienated from our faith... *(Invite participants to name specific people.)*

*All:*
We praise you, O Lord.

*Presider:*
For those in our world who work for peace and try to make all feel welcome... *(Invite participants to name specific people.)*

*All:*
We praise you, O Lord.

*Presider:*
For our community gathered here and all good gifts we share with one another... *(Invite participants to name specific people.)*

*All:*
We praise you, O Lord.

Invite participants to share their own intentions. Follow each with:

*All:*
We praise you, O Lord.

**Concluding Rite**

*Presider:*
Recognizing God's goodness, let us join together and pray:

*All:*
Our Father... Amen.

*Presider:*
Let us bow our heads and ask for God's blessing:

May the God of all caring always hold you in the palm of God's hand. May Christ, the Good Shepherd, carry you gently on his shoulders. May the Spirit enflame your lives with confidence and affirmation. And may we all be blessed, Father, Son and Holy Spirit.

*All:*
Amen.

Invite participants to exchange a Sign of Peace.

**Concluding Song**
Sing together "All Are Welcome" or "Working for the Lord."

**2:25 pm** Evaluation
See the Introduction, page 4.

**2:30 pm** Departure and Team Meeting
See the Introduction, pages 2 and 4.

**Note:** Remember to mail participants' letters (Journal #7).

# TOUGH EMOTIONS RETREATS

## RETREAT #8:
### Overnight Model: Tough Emotions

## GETTING READY

### Focus
Retreat #8 combines elements of Retreats #5, 6 and 7 to take a broad look at several tough emotions faced by today's teens, including stress, depression, anger, hatred and insecurity. Participants not only explore the ways these emotions are expressed, but search for healthy ways to cope with them, both through their relationship with God and their relationships with one another.

### Core Questions
- What is stress? depression? anger? hatred? insecurity?
- How do these emotions impact us?
- What are some of the unhealthy ways we try to cope with these difficult emotions?
- In what healthy, constructive ways can we cope with these emotions?
- What help does scripture offer when dealing with these emotions?
- How can we help each other survive these tough emotions?

### Overview
*first day:*

| | |
|---|---|
| 6:00 pm | Team Arrives for Set-Up and Team Meeting |
| 7:00 pm | Participants Arrive |
| 7:15 pm | Welcome: Team Introductions, Rules and Overview of the Day |
| 7:30 pm | Session 1: Community Building |
| 8:30 pm | Snack Break and Team Check-In |
| 8:45 pm | Session 2: Stressed Out and D-Pressed! |
| 9:45 pm | Session 3: Let's *Un*stress! |
| 10:30 pm | Social Time and Team Check-In |
| 11:30 pm | Compline |
| 12:00 am | Bedtime |
| 12:30 am | Lights Out |

*second day:*

| | |
|---|---|
| 8:30 am | Wake-Up |
| 9:00 am | Breakfast |
| 9:45 am | Morning Prayer |
| 10:15 am | Session 4: Getting Mad, Getting Even |
| 12:00 pm | Lunch and Team Check-In |
| 1:00 pm | Session 5: Seeing Ourselves as God Sees Us |
| 2:30 pm | Snack Break and Team Check-In |
| 3:00 pm | Session 6: Affirmation |
| 4:30 pm | Closing Ritual |
| 5:00 pm | Departure and Team Meeting |

### Materials
*for the retreat:*
- copies of *Quick Takes for Teens*, Volume 2, 1 per Team Leader
- Bibles
- name-tag supplies
- newsprint
- colored felt markers
- masking tape
- paper lunch bags
- slips of paper

- art supplies (paper and crayons, construction paper, glue, glitter, modeling clay, etc.)
- construction toys (Tinker Toys®, Legos®, Toobers and Zots®, etc.)
- three-hole folders, 1 per participant
- colored paper or paper with pre-printed designs
- three-hole punch
- photocopies of Journal Sheets #5 (page 104), #6 (page 105), #7 (page 106) and #8 (page 107), 1 for each per participant
- photocopies of the Evaluation (page 114), 1 per participant
- pens or pencils
- paper
- index cards
- hat or basket
- discarded watch (or other item of value)
- block of wood
- hammer
- pipe cleaners/chenille craft wires
- CD player
- quiet CDs appropriate for break and reflection times, and to use in the activity "Unstress" in Session 3
- food and beverages for breaks and meals

*for the ritual:*
In the Advance Preparation Checklist, below, you will be asked to choose two rituals for this retreat from Retreats #5, 6 and 7. The materials you will need for those Rituals will be found in the Materials list for those retreats.

## Advance Preparation Checklist

- ☐ Set the date and reserve the site. Check both school and parish calendars!
- ☐ Read through the Retreat Plan. Decide which activities to include, substitute, adapt, etc.
- ☐ Recruit and train the Retreat Team. See page 1 of the Introduction.
- ☐ Recruit a Team Member to give the Witness Talk in Session 5. Beside the basic guidelines given in the Introduction (page 2), suggest to the Team Member:
  — In your talk, reflect on Romans 8:31-39.
  — Share a personal experience of fear and insecurity, and what gave you the courage the believe in yourself.
- ☐ Choose two of the Rituals from Retreat 5 (page 34, on Stress and Depression), Retreat 6 (page 40, on Anger and Hatred) and Retreat 7 (page 45, on Insecurity and Self-Esteem), one to use for Morning Prayer and one for the Closing Ritual. Also decide who will preside at these rituals. Ask the presider to prepare the Reflection to be given in each ritual. Specific suggestions for these Reflections are given in the corresponding Advance Preparation Checklist in each of the three retreats.
- ☐ Prepare the roleplay cards for the activity "Self-Esteem Roleplay" in Session 5. For directions, see *Quick Takes for Teens*, Volume 2, page 46.
- ☐ Create Retreat Journals for each participant:
  — Photocopy Journal Sheets #5, #6, #7 and #8.
  — Alternate the Journal Sheets with sheets of blank paper.
  — Three-hole punch all sheets and bind them in three-hole folders.
  — For visual interest, use colorful paper or paper with pre-printed designs, available at office supply stores.
- ☐ Recruit a guest speaker to join you for a presentation on hate crimes as part of the activity "What Hath Anger Wrought?" in Session 4. For suggestions, see the instructions for the activity in *Quick Takes for Teens*, Volume 2, page 12.
- ☐ Arrange for food and beverages.
- ☐ Arrange for transportation, as necessary.
- ☐ Get permission slips, as necessary.
- ☐ Photocopy the Evaluations.
- ☐ Collect and pack materials.
- ☐ Envision the environment and prepare necessary materials. See page 3 of the Introduction.
- ☐ Pre-assign participants to small groups. Assign a Team Member to facilitate each group. Determine locations for small-group discussions.

## RETREAT PLAN

*first day:*
**6:00 pm** Team Arrives for Set-Up and Team Meeting
See the Introduction, page 2.

**7:00 pm** Participants Arrive

**Name Tags**
See the Introduction, page 3.

**7:15 pm** Welcome
See the Introduction, pages 3-4.

**Team Introductions**
*(5 minutes)*

**Rules and Overview of the Day**
*(5 minutes)*

**Distribution of Journals**
*(5 minutes)*
Distribute pens or pencils and the Retreat Journals prepared before the retreat. Explain:
- Throughout the retreat, feel free to use the blank pages in your Retreat Journal to record your feelings, thoughts, ideas and reaction.
- Two of the Journal Sheets—#6 and #8—will be used in activities we will do together.
- The remaining two Journal Sheets—#5 and #7—are yours to use as you wish.
- Please put your name on the front of your folder, to help you keep track of it.

If time allows, you could invite participants to list on one of the blank pages of their Retreat Journals two or three hopes they have for the retreat. Ask volunteers to share what they have written.

**7:30 pm** Session 1: Community Building
We suggest that you select from the following icebreakers, but be certain to complete "Star Bags," the final activity listed, because the "Star Bags" are used throughout the retreat. In addition to "Star Bags," feel free to add your favorite icebreaker or choose others from *Quick Takes for Teens*, Volume 2, pages 6-7.

**Picture Your Week**
*(15 minutes)*
See *Quick Takes for Teens*, Volume 2, page 7.

**Emotion Walk**
*(10 minutes)*
Invite group members to stand in a large circle. Recruit a volunteer to stand in the middle of the circle. Explain:
- As a group, start walking clockwise around the circle.
- Once we start walking, I'll call out a feeling. When I've named the feeling, start walking *as if you were feeling that feeling*. Let your movements, posture and facial expressions reflect the feeling I've named.
- After a few seconds, I'll call out another feeling. Change your walk to reflect that new feeling.

Here are several emotions to name; add others if you wish, or invite volunteers to call out other emotions for group members to mirror:
- anger
- love
- loneliness
- happiness
- hate
- fear
- insecurity

**Emotion Talk**
*(20 minutes)*
See *Quick Takes for Teens*, Volume 2, page 39.

Only use "Emotion Talk" if you first complete "Emotion Walk."

**The Insecurity Song**
*(15 minutes)*
See *Quick Takes for Teens*, Volume 2, page 43.

**Star Bags**
*(15 minutes)*

Distribute pens or pencils and a paper bag to each participant. Make available the assortment of craft materials, slips of paper, construction paper and felt markers. Explain to participants:

- Create a Star Bag for yourself.
- First put your name somewhere on your bag.
- Then decorate your bag as you wish using the available materials.
- When we've finished, we will put our bags together somewhere in the room. *(Choose a place where they will be safe, but accessible.)*
- Throughout the weekend, add affirmations to people's bags—each written on a slip of paper—as you think of things you appreciate about those people.

**8:30 pm** Snack Break and Team Check-In
See the Introduction, page 2.

**8:45 pm** Session 2: Stressed-Out and D-Pressed!

### Stress Evaluation
*(15 minutes)*
See *Quick Takes for Teens*, Volume 2, page 19.

### Stress Response
*(15 minutes)*
See *Quick Takes for Teens*, Volume 2, page 20.

### Human Gumby®
*(10 minutes)*
See *Quick Takes for Teens*, Volume 2, page 23.

### Understanding Depression
*(15 minutes)*
See *Quick Takes for Teens*, Volume 2, page 19.

### Stretch Break
*(5 minutes)*
Give group members a brief break while you prepare for the next session.

**9:45 pm** Session 3: Let's *Un*stress!

### Coping
*(15 minutes)*
See *Quick Takes for Teens*, Volume 2, page 18.

### Unstress
*(15 minutes)*
See *Quick Takes for Teens*, Volume 2, page 18.

### The Bigger Picture
*(15 minutes)*
See *Quick Takes for Teens*, Volume 2, page 21.

**10:30 pm** Social Time and Team Check-In
See the Introduction, page 2.

**11:30 pm** Compline
See the Introduction, pages 6-7, and the Advance Preparation Checklist, above.

**12:00 am** Bedtime

**12:30 am** Lights Out

*second day:*
**8:30 am** Wake-Up

**9:00 am** Breakfast

**9:45 am** Morning Prayer
See the Introduction, pages 6-7, and the Advance Preparation Checklist, above.

**10:15 am** Session 4: Getting Mad, Getting Even

### Smash It!
*(10 minutes)*
See *Quick Takes for Teens*, Volume 2, page 8.

### Examining Anger
*(20 minutes)*
See *Quick Takes for Teens*, Volume 2, page 9.

### Journal Reflection
*(20 minutes)*
Distribute pens or pencils and invite participants to work individually to complete Journal #8, found in their Retreat Journals.

After about 10 minutes, regather and invite volunteers to share their insights with the group.

### Anger Symbols, Part I
*(10 minutes)*
See *Quick Takes for Teens*, Volume 2, page 12.
At the conclusion of the activity, invite participants to place their symbols together in a safe place somewhere in the meeting space. Participants return to the symbols later in the session.

### Stretch Break
*(5 minutes)*
Give group members a brief break before continuing with the session.

### What Hath Anger Wrought?
*(30 minutes)*
See *Quick Takes for Teens*, Volume 2, page 12.

### Anger Symbols, Part II
*(10 minutes)*
Explain to participants:
- Retrieve your anger symbols.
- What step can you take toward resolving the anger represented by your symbol? Think of a way, not to dismiss or discount it, but to embrace it and begin working through it in a healthy way. Is your next step forgiveness? confrontation? honesty? awareness?
- Change your symbol—removing something, adding something or reshaping it—to reflect this next step you could take.

After 5 minutes of individual work, regather and invite volunteers to show and explain their altered symbols to the group.

**12:00 pm** Lunch and Team Check-In
See the Introduction, page 2.

**1:00 pm** Session 5: Seeing Ourselves as God Sees Us

### Self-Esteem Roleplay
*(30 minutes)*
See *Quick Takes for Teens*, Volume 2, page 46.

### Self-Esteem Killers
*(10 minutes)*
See *Quick Takes for Teens*, Volume 2, page 47.

Refocus the group's attention and introduce the Witness Talk Team member.

### Witness Talk
*(10 minutes)*
See the Introduction, page 2, and the Advance Preparation Checklist.

### Stretch Break
*(15 minutes)*
Give group members a brief break before continuing with the session.

### Let's Pretend, Part I
*(10 minutes)*
See *Quick Takes for Teens*, Volume 2, page 42.

### Star Bag Affirmations, Part I
*(15 minutes)*
Invite participants to spend the next 15 minutes writing affirmations and self-esteem boosters for one another. They sign

and place the affirmations in the appropriate Star Bags created earlier in the retreat.

Provide, as necessary, additional slips of paper and make available pens and pencils. Suggest that participants could:
- Let people know you appreciate things that they have shared.
- Let people know you enjoy some aspect of who they are.
- Thank someone for a kind word or comforting touch.
- Give encouragement to someone going through a rough time.

Discourage people from reading the contents of their Star Bags. They will be asked to read their affirmations after the retreat ends.

**2:30 pm**  Snack Break and Team Check-In
See Introduction, page 2.

**3:00 pm**  Session 6: Affirmation

### Let's Pretend, Part II
*(15 minutes)*
See *Quick Takes for Teens*, Volume 2, page 43.

### Secure
*(30 minutes)*
See *Quick Takes for Teens*, Volume 2, page 39.

### Stretch Break
*(15 minutes)*
Give group members a break before continuing with the session.

### Journal Reflection
*(15 minutes)*
Distribute pens or pencils and invite participants to work individually to complete Journal #6, found in their Retreat Journals.

After about 10 minutes, regather and invite volunteers to share their letters with the group. After sharing, ask participants to remove their letters from their Retreat Journals, insert them in their envelopes and stamp and address their envelopes. Collect these to mail to participants a few weeks after the retreat.

### Star Bag Affirmations, Part II
*(15 minutes)*
Invite participants to spend another 15 minutes writing affirmations and self-esteem boosters for one another, as they have done earlier in the retreat. This time, encourage them to remember people whom they might have skipped before.

Again, discourage people from reading the contents of their Star Bags until after the retreat ends.

**4:30 pm**  Closing Ritual
See the Advance Preparation Checklist, above.

**4:55 pm**  Evaluation
See the Introduction, page 4.

**5:00 pm**  Departure and Team Meeting
See the Introduction, pages 2 and 4.

**Note:** Remember to mail participants' letters!

# CHAPTER 3

## RETREAT #9:
### MEDIA MANIA

## GETTING READY

### Focus
Retreat #9 explores the influence—both obvious and subtle—of contemporary media. Participants take a deeper, critical look at television, music, movies, advertising and the Internet, then consider ways to reduce the power of the media in their lives.

### Core Questions
- How influential *is* the media?
- Why does contemporary media exist?
- What special "tricks" does the media use to influence us? to sell to us?
- What choices can we make in the face of a constant flood of media images and noise?

### Overview
| | |
|---|---|
| 8:00 am | Team Arrives for Set-Up and Team Meeting |
| 9:00 am | Participants Arrive |
| 9:15 am | Welcome: Team Introductions, Rules and Overview of the Day |
| 9:30 am | Session 1: Community Building |
| 10:15 am | Snack Break and Team Check-In |
| 10:30 am | Session 2: The Boob Tube |
| 11:30 am | Lunch and Team Check-In |
| 12:15 pm | Session 3: Digging for the Truth |
| 1:15 pm | Session 4: How Can We Influence Media? |
| 2:00 pm | Closing Ritual: God's Peace in a Noisy World |
| 2:25 pm | Evaluation |
| 2:30 pm | Departure and Team Meeting |

### Materials
*for the retreat:*
- copies of *Quick Takes for Teens*, Volume 3, 1 per Team Leader
- Bibles
- name-tag supplies
- newsprint
- colored felt markers
- masking tape
- photocopies of Journal #9 (page 108), 1 per participant
- photocopies of the Evaluation (page 114), 1 per participant
- pens or pencils
- videotapes prepared in advance by several retreat participants (See the Advance Preparation Checklist, below.)
- video sampler (See the Advance Preparation Checklist, below.)
- TV and VCR
- examples of entertainment options available to teenagers (See the Advance Preparation Checklist, below.)
- 2 large sheets of poster board
- scissors
- recent magazines geared for youth and/or dealing with fashion or fitness
- glue sticks
- CD player
- CDs appropriate for break and reflection times
- food and beverages for breaks and lunch

*for the ritual:*
- recorded or printed music:
  — "Now" by Rory Cooney (GIA) or "Lead Us to the Water; Gathering" by Tom Kendzia (OCP)

- a musical setting of Psalm 139 that is familiar to you community
- the refrain of "Hiding Place" by Liam Lawton (GIA) or the refrain of "We Will Praise You" by Tom Kendzia (OCP)
- "May God Grant You a Blessing" (Swahili folk hymn, GIA) or "Lead Us to the Water; Dismissal" by Tom Kendzia (OCP)

■ candle
■ matches
■ cassette tape player
■ cassette tape recording of a television newscast, mixed with loud music with "negative" lyrics
■ recent newspapers with headlines reflecting current disaster and suffering
■ popular "teen" magazines

## Advance Preparation Checklist

☐ Set the date and reserve the site. Check both school and parish calendars!

☐ Read through the Retreat Plan. Decide which activities to include, substitute, adapt, etc.

☐ Recruit and train the Retreat Team. See page 1 of the Introduction.

☐ Invite several participants to bring videotapes of what they consider to be entertaining television programming. Each tape should include no more than 5 minutes of material. Ask participants *not* to bring anything potentially offensive due to language, sex or violence.

☐ Prepare a video sampler of 10 minutes of television: commercial, parts of a music video, a segment of a popular sitcom or soap opera, etc.

☐ Collect examples or symbols of entertainment options available for teens, for example, a concert ticket stub, a novel, a CD, a teen-oriented magazine, a video game cartridge, etc.

☐ Decide who will preside at the Closing Ritual. Ask the presider to prepare the Reflection to be given in the ritual, reflecting on Colossians 3:1-48-14 and sharing thoughts on the relationship of media (movies, books, magazines, TV, video games, the Internet, etc.) and faith. The following questions also may help in preparation:
  — What in the media (in all its different forms) *hinders* our relationship with God or with each other? *helps* these relationships?
  — How can we overcome "media madness," more fully opening our lives to the presence of God?
  — In what ways can we let the media call us to be God's presence for others?

As a part of the Reflection, the presider may wish to have the assembly reflect on any one of these same questions, either silently or in groups of no more than three members each.

☐ Recruit volunteers to help with the "media cacophony" in the Ritual Action portion of the Closing Ritual:
  — Ask one volunteer to either play (on the piano or using a recording) "Now" or "Lead Us to the Water; Gathering" at a moderate, consistent volume.
  — Ask a second volunteer to play the cassette tape of a television newscast and "negative" music, quietly at first, then slowly increasing the volume until it overwhelms the other music.
  — Ask several other volunteers each to simultaneously read headlines from both the newspapers and the teen magazines, quietly at first, then slowly increasing in volume.

The combined "noise" increases in volume until annoying and grating; at this point the leader signals for all music and voices to stop, resulting in a surprising, relief-filled silence. Arrange to practice this process with the volunteers before the retreat.

☐ Recruit a Team Member to give the Witness Talk in Session 4. Besides the basic guidelines given in the Introduction (page 2), suggest to the Team Member:
  — In your talk, reflect on Colossians 3:1-17. What do you think Paul—the writer of Colossians—would want us to understand about the media if he were around today to see its influence?
  — Share a personal experience of the power—for good or ill—of the media.

☐ Arrange for food and beverages.

☐ Arrange for transportation, as necessary.

- ☐ Get permission slips, as necessary.
- ☐ Photocopy necessary materials, for example, Journal Sheets and Evaluations.
- ☐ Collect and pack materials.
- ☐ Envision the environment and prepare necessary materials. See the Introduction, page 2.
- ☐ Pre-assign participants to small groups. Assign a Team Member to facilitate each group. Determine locations for small-group discussions.

## RETREAT PLAN

**8:00 am** Team Arrives for Set-Up and Team Meeting
See the Introduction, page 2.

**9:00 am** Participants Arrive

### Name Tags
See the Introduction, page 3, or *Quick Takes for Teens*, Volume 3, page 7.

**9:15 am** Welcome
See the Introduction, pages 3-4.

### Team Introductions
*(5 minutes)*

### Rules
*(5 minutes)*

### Overview of the Day
*(5 minutes)*

**9:30 am** Session 1: Community Building
We suggest the following icebreaker. Add your favorites or choose others from *Quick Takes for Teens*, Volume 3, pages 6-7.

### Song Rewrite
*(20 minutes)*
See *Quick Takes for Teens*, Volume 3, page 6.

**10:15 am** Snack Break and Team Check-In
See the Introduction, page 2.

**10:30 am** Session 2: The Boob Tube

### Gluttony or Entertainment?
*(25 minutes)*
See *Quick Takes for Teens*, Volume 3, page 16.

### Journal Reflection
*(15 minutes)*
Distribute pens or pencils and photocopies of Journal #9. Invite participants to work individually to complete the sheet.

After about 10 minutes, regather and invite volunteers to share their insights with the group.

### Television Mesmerism
*(20 minutes)*
See *Quick Takes for Teens*, Volume 3, page 19.

**11:30 am** Lunch and Team Check-In
See the Introduction, page 2.

**12:15 pm** Session 3: Digging for the Truth

### Behind the Hype
*(20 minutes)*
See *Quick Takes for Teens*, Volume 3, page 26.

### Who Am I Supposed to Be?
*(20 minutes)*
See *Quick Takes for Teens*, Volume 3, page 22.

### What's Normal?
*(15 minutes)*
See *Quick Takes for Teens*, Volume 3, page 24.

**Stretch Break**
*(5 minutes)*
Give group members a brief break while you prepare for the next session.

**1:15 pm**   Session 4: How Can We Influence the Media?

**The Movie I Would Make**
*(15 minutes)*
See *Quick Takes for Teens*, Volume 3, page 22.

Refocus the group's attention and introduce the Witness Talk Team Member.

**Witness Talk**
*(10 minutes)*
See the Introduction, page 2 and the Advance Preparation Checklist, above.

**Talk Show Mania**
*(20 minutes)*
See *Quick Takes for Teens*, Volume 3, page 21.

# Ritual

**2:00 pm**   Closing Ritual: God's Peace in a Noisy World

**Gathering Song**
Sing together "Now" or "Lead Us to the Water; Gathering."

**Introductory Rite**

*Presider:*
In the name of the Father, of the Son and of the Holy Spirit.

*All:*
Amen.

*Presider:*
The Lord be with you.

*All:*
And also with you.

*Presider:*
In this age of music, television, radio and computers we need to find time for silence, time for God to speak to us in the quietness of our hearts. Now is the time for us to seek salvation and peace from a God who can deliver us from the problems of this world.

Let us pray. *(silence)*

Lord Jesus, you are the source of hope in a darkened world. Lord, have mercy.

*All:*
Lord, have mercy.

*Presider:*
Christ Jesus, you are the light that helps us focus on the true needs of this world. Christ, have mercy.

*All:*
Christ, have mercy

*Presider:*
Lord Jesus, you are our peace in a world assaulting us with noise. Lord, have mercy.

*All:*
Lord, have mercy.

*Presider:*
May almighty God have mercy on us, forgive us our sins and bring us to everlasting life.

*All:*
>Amen.

**Scripture**
Read aloud Colossians 3:1-4.

**Psalm**
Sing a setting of Psalm 139.

**Reflection**
The presider shares thoughts on the relationship of media (movies, books, magazines, TV, video games, the Internet, etc.) and faith. See the Introduction, page 5, and the Advance Preparation Checklist, above.

**Ritual Action**
Begin the "media cacophony" described in the Advance Preparation Checklist, above, and as practiced before the Retreat.

In the silence that follows the signal to stop the "media cacophony," light the candle, reread the scripture and begin the litany.

**Litany of Peace**
Participants sing the response, either the refrain of "Hiding Place" or the refrain of "We Will Praise You."

*Presider:*
>For peace...

*All:*
>(sung response)

*Presider:*
>For an outpouring of love...

*All:*
>(sung response)

*Presider:*
>For comfort and safety...

*All:*
>(sung response)

*Presider:*
>For wisdom and peace of heart in the Word of God...

*All:*
>(sung response)

**Closing Rite**
*Presider:*
>Let us pray in the words Christ himself has given us:

*All:*
>Our Father... Amen.

*Presider:*
>The Lord be with you.

*All:*
>And also with you.

*Presider:*
>Let us bow our heads and ask for God's blessing:

>May God's peace be all around us.

*All:*
>Amen.

*Presider:*
>May Christ's peace flow to those in need.

*All:*
>Amen.

*Presider:*
>May the Holy Spirit guide us in paths of peace.

*All:*
  Amen.

*Presider:*
  And may we be blessed, Father, Son and Holy Spirit.

*All:*
  Amen.

Invite participants to exchange a Sign of Peace.

**Closing Song**
Sing together "May God Grant You a Blessing" or "Lead Us to the Water; Dismissal."

**2:25 pm** Evaluation
See the Introduction, page 4.

**2:30 pm** Departure and Team Meeting
See the Introduction, pages 2 and 4.

# RETREAT #10:
## GLOBAL CONCERNS

## GETTING READY

### Focus
Retreat #10 encourages participants to explore several world problems, specifically the environment, violence and AIDS. In each session, participants first examine the scope of one of the problems, then discuss possible ways to help alleviate the problem.

### Core Questions
- What environmental problems threaten the future of our planet?
- How can we become part of the solution—instead of the problem—when it comes to environmental issues?
- How does violence impact our families, schools, communities and world?
- What can we do to help stop the violence around us?
- In what ways does AIDS impact its victims?
- How can we help those with AIDS, their families and friends?
- In general, how can we bring healing to a hurting world?

### Overview
| | |
|---|---|
| 8:00 am | Team Arrives for Set-Up and Team Meeting |
| 9:00 am | Participants Arrive |
| 9:15 am | Welcome: Team Introductions, Rules and Overview of the Day |
| 9:30 am | Session 1: Community Building |
| 10:15 am | Snack Break and Team Check-In |
| 10:30 am | Session 2: The Environment |
| 11:30 am | Lunch and Team Check-In |
| 12:15 pm | Session 3: Violence |
| 1:15 pm | Session 4: AIDS |
| 2:00 pm | Closing Ritual: From Hurting to Healing |
| 2:25 pm | Evaluation |
| 2:30 pm | Departure and Team Meeting |

### Materials
*for the retreat:*
- copies of *Quick Takes for Teens*, Volume 3, 1 per Team Leader
- Bibles
- name-tag supplies
- newsprint
- colored felt markers
- masking tape
- paper
- photocopies of Journal #10 (page 109), 1 per participant
- photocopies of the Evaluation (page 114), 1 per participant
- pens or pencils
- index cards
- 1-3 large (4' or 5'), white, weather balloons (available from Andon Balloons, 66th and 12th Ave., Richfield, MN 55423, 1-800-479-5795)
- 1-3 slide projectors
- 1-3 50' extension cords
- slides of:
  — creation images
  — faces of people of all ages
  — faces of participants on the retreat
  — printed words related to creation and people
- 3' heavy cotton string

59

- duct tape
- air pump or vacuum cleaner with reversible hose
- TV and VCR
- video sampler of television violence (See the Advance Preparation Checklist, below.)
- printed information on AIDS (See the Advance Preparation Checklist, below.)
- CD player
- CDs appropriate for break and reflection times
- food and beverages for breaks and lunch

*for the ritual:*
- recorded or printed music:
  — "Over My Head" (traditional, African-American, GIA and OCP)
  — a musical setting of Psalm 23 that is familiar to your community
  — "Yes, Lord" by Donna Peña (GIA) or "Go and Make a Difference" by Steve Agrisano (OCP)

## Advance Preparation Checklist

- [ ] Set the date and reserve the site. Check both school and parish calendars!
- [ ] Read through the Retreat Plan. Decide which activities to include, substitute, adapt, etc.
- [ ] Recruit and train the Retreat Team. See the Introduction, page 1.
- [ ] Prepare a video sampler of television violence. Keep segments to 30 seconds or less and include clips from a variety of shows, including the news, so-called "reality shows," sports, music videos, TV dramas and cartoons.
- [ ] Decide who will preside at the Closing Ritual.
- [ ] Call the National AIDS Hotline at 1-800-342-AIDS and request pamphlets about AIDS written for teenagers. Or contact your local health department for current information on AIDS and AIDS prevention.
- [ ] Recruit a guest speaker to give the Reflection during the ritual. Look for someone who has worked to bring healing in one of the areas covered in today's retreat: the environment, violence or AIDS. Invite the speaker to share from his or her own experience. The following questions also may help in preparation:
  — From your understanding of scripture, how would Jesus address this issue?
  — In your own life, what inspired you to do the type of work you do on behalf of the environment (*or* in trying to stop violence, in ministering to those with AIDS, etc.)?
  — What behaviors or attitudes do *we* need to overcome to positively affect the environment, reduce violence or help stop AIDS?
  As a part of the Reflection, the speaker may wish to have the assembly reflect on any one of these same questions, either silently or in groups of no more than three members each.
- [ ] Recruit a Team Member to give the Witness Talk in Session 4. Besides the basic guidelines given in the Introduction (page 2), suggest to the Team Member:
  — In your talk, reflect on 2 Corinthians 5:17-21. What do you think Paul—the writer of this letter—thinks is a cure for violence?
  — Share a personal experience of violence, the impact it had on you or someone you care about, and how you dealt with it.
- [ ] Arrange for food and beverages.
- [ ] Arrange for transportation, as necessary.
- [ ] Get permission slips, as necessary.
- [ ] Photocopy necessary materials, for example, Journal Sheets and Evaluations.
- [ ] For the activity Weather Balloon, in Session 2:
  — For each balloon to be used in the activity gather one slide tray or carousel of 30-40 slides of creation images, printed words related to creation and faces of people—including, but not limited to, retreat participants.
  — Recruit three volunteers for each balloon to be used in the activity:
    • One will hold and release a balloon.
    • One will hold a slide projector on his or her shoulder and project slides onto the balloon as participants move the balloon around the room.
    • One will follow the projectionist, holding the extension cord and keeping it out of the way.

— Select an appropriate song to play during the activity. Choose a song about creation, about working together or about supporting each other.
— Just before the retreat, for each balloon, connect an extension cord to a projector and secure the connection with duct tape.
— About 1-2 hours before the activity, inflate the balloons until they are firm *but not tight*. Tie each balloon with about a foot of cotton string. The balloons are fragile, so handle carefully and store them away from sharp objects.

☐ Collect and pack materials.
☐ Envision the environment and prepare necessary materials. See the Introduction, page 2.
☐ Pre-assign participants to small groups. Assign a Team Member to facilitate each group. Determine locations for small-group discussions.

## RETREAT PLAN

**8:00 am** Team Arrives for Set-Up and Team Meeting
See the Introduction, page 2.

**9:00 am** Participants Arrive

### Name Tags
See the Introduction, page 3, or *Quick Takes for Teens*, Volume 3, page 7.

**9:15 am** Welcome
See the Introduction, pages 3-4.

### Team Introductions
(5 minutes)

### Rules
(5 minutes)

### Overview of the Day
(5 minutes)

**9:30 am** Session 1: Community Building
We suggest the following icebreaker. Add your favorites or choose others from *Quick Takes for Teens*, Volume 3, pages 6-7.

### If I Could...
(20 minutes)
See *Quick Takes for Teens*, Volume 3, page 7.

**10:15 am** Snack Break and Team Check-In
See the Introduction, page 2.

**10:30 am** Session 2: The Environment

### An Environmental Thing
(20 minutes)
See *Quick Takes for Teens*, Volume 3, page 9.

### God and The Environment
(20 minutes)
See *Quick Takes for Teens*, Volume 3, page 10.

### Weather Balloon
(20 minutes)
Invite group members to imagine that the balloons represent all of God's creation, including all of humanity. Explain that they will gently toss the balloons from person to person throughout the room, reverencing the balloons as if participants themselves were responsible for holding creation in their own hands. Ask participants to remove sharp objects (watches, rings, etc.) and to use the palms of their hands to keep the balloon aloft, avoiding sharp fingernails and sharp obstacles around the room (light fixtures, sprinkler heads, pipes, etc.).

Gently launch the balloons. At the same time, turn on the music, turn out the lights and start the projectors. It is possible that a balloon will burst accidentally, or that one will burst because of intentional disregard or foolishness. Pay attention to what happens in the group. When the song has finished, retrieve the balloons and secure them safely. Discuss:

- What did you see happening in this activity?
- How well did we "care for creation"?
- How has this activity demonstrated how society cares for creation? for other people?
- What are some of the "sharp objects" that harm creation? humanity?

**Note:** This activity is meant to be fun and uplifting. Too many rules or too much concern for the welfare of the balloons weakens the impact. Set the tone for imaging care for creation and humanity, but let the group experience the activity as it unfolds. If one or all of the balloons burst, use this as a teachable moment about the fragility of creation and the human condition.

**11:30 am** Lunch and Team Check-In
See the Introduction, page 2.

**12:15 pm** Session 3: Violence

### Horror Snippets
See *Quick Takes for Teens,* Volume 3, page 43.
*(15 minutes)*

### Marketing Violence
See *Quick Takes for Teens,* Volume 3, page 41.
*(15 minutes)*

### Journal Reflection
*(15 minutes)*
Distribute pens or pencils, Bibles and photocopies of Journal #10. Invite participants to work individually to complete the sheet.

After about 10 minutes, regather and invite volunteers to share their stories with the group.

Refocus the group's attention and introduce the Witness Talk Team member.

### Witness Talk
*(10 minutes)*
See the Introduction, page 2, and the Advance Preparation Checklist, above.

### Stretch Break
*(5 minutes)*
Give group members a brief break while you prepare for the next session.

**1:15 pm** Session 4: AIDS

### AIDS Graffiti
*(10 minutes)*
See *Quick Takes for Teens,* Volume 3, page 8.

### AIDS Accounts
*(15 minutes)*
See *Quick Takes for Teens,* Volume 3, page 11.

### Aiding People with AIDS
*(20 minutes)*
See *Quick Takes for Teens,* Volume 3, page 12.

# Ritual

**2:00 pm** Closing Ritual: From Hurting to Healing

**Gathering Song**
Sing together "Over my Head."

**Introductory Rite**

*Presider:*
In the name of the Father, Son and Holy Spirit.

*All:*
Amen.

*Presider:*
The Lord be with you.

*All:*
And also with you.

*Presider:*
As we gather, let us look at ourselves as people of healing. Let us challenge ourselves to work toward ways of restoring the environment, ending violence and healing AIDS.

Let us first name those places where there is hurt in the world:

Invite participants to name places where they see the need for healing in the world. They can name specific issues related to today's three topics — the environment, violence and AIDS — or any other issues that concern them. As they do so, let the song "Over My Head" play softly in the background.

When all who wish to name needs have done so, continue:

*Presider:*
For all the hurts of the world, we confidently proclaim that our God is in charge, and that healing flows from him, through us, to others. So together we sing...

Sing together "Over my Head."

**Scripture**
Read aloud 2 Corinthians 5:17-21.

**Psalm**
Sing a setting of Psalm 23.

**Reflection**
Invite the guest speaker to share. See the Introduction, page 5, and the Advance Preparation Checklist, above.

**Ritual Action**
Begin by asking participants to stand together in one large circle. Invite them to hold their hands in front of them, palms up. Explain:

- Each of us will have a few moments to offer a silent blessing to every other person in the circle.
- A blessing could ask God to:
  — heal where the person currently is hurting
  — help the person bring healing to a hurting world

Demonstrate the following:

- Step forward and turn to face the person on your right (Person A).
- Place your hands, palm down, on their hands, palm up.
- Silently pray a blessing for Person A.
- When finished, move to the next person in the circle (Person B) and repeat.
- When finished, move to the next person (Person C) and repeat; meanwhile, Person A steps forward and turns to face Person B, offering Person B a blessing, just as you did.
- When you move to Person D, Person A will move to Person C. When you move to Person E, Person A will move to Person D, and Person B will bless Person C.
- Continue in this way, until all people in the circle have offered a blessing for all other members of the circle. Note that when you return to your original place in the circle, all other members of the circle will eventually pass you, offering their blessings.

If you have a larger group—over 25, for example—considering dividing into two or more smaller groups for this Ritual Action.

When all have participants have offered blessings to all others, continue with the Litany of Healing.

**Litany of Healing**
Participants sing the response, either the refrain of "Yes, My Lord" of the refrain of "Go and Make a Difference."

*Presider:*
Having been called by God to be people of healing, let us lift up prayers of praise for people who have brought healing to a hurting world.

For men and women of our world who have worked to save God's creation—

Pause to allow participants to suggest names.

*All:*
(sung response)

*Presider:*
For men and women of our church who have shown us the way of peace—

Pause to allow participants to add other names.

*All:*
(sung response)

*Presider:*
For those people and organizations who work to relieve the suffering of AIDS and other devastating illnesses—

Pause to allow participants to add other names.

*All:*
(sung response)

**Concluding Rite**
*Presider:*
Jesus showed us the true way of healing. Let us join in the words that Christ himself has given us:

*All:*
Our Father... Amen.

*Presider:*
The Lord be with you.

*All:*
And also with you.

*Presider:*
Let us bow our heads and ask for God's blessing:

May the Lord bless and keep you, may Christ's face shine upon you and may the Holy Spirit guide you in healing the hurting world, Father, Son and Holy Spirit.

*All:*
Amen.

Invite participants to exchange a Sign of Peace.

**Closing Song**
Sing together all of "Yes, Lord" or all of "Go and Make a Difference."

**2:25 pm** Evaluation
See the Introduction, page 4.

**2:30 pm** Departure and Team Meeting
See the Introduction, pages 2 and 4.

# WORLD PROBLEMS RETREATS

## RETREAT #11:
### Poverty and Wealth

## GETTING READY

### Focus
Retreat #11 invites participants to explore the complex issues of wealth and poverty, hunger and homelessness, taking a look at both the needs of the those around them and their own attitudes and behaviors.

### Core Questions
- What problems are caused by the great disparity between the poor and the wealthy?
- In what ways do our attitudes about money and possessions impact our families? our communities? our friendships? our relationship with God?
- What guidance does scripture offer for the use of wealth? the need to help the poor? the hungry? the homeless?
- How can we tune in to God's will for us when it comes to money and "things"?

### Overview
| | |
|---|---|
| 8:00 am | Team Arrives for Set-Up and Team Meeting |
| 9:00 am | Participants Arrive |
| 9:15 am | Welcome: Team Introductions, Rules and Overview of the Day |
| 9:30 am | Session 1: Community Building |
| 10:15 am | Snack Break and Team Check-In |
| 10:30 am | Session 2: Hunger |
| 11:30 am | Lunch and Team Check-In |
| 12:15 pm | Session 3: Homelessness |
| 1:15 pm | Session 4: What Can I Do? |
| 2:00 pm | Closing Ritual: Justice, Peace and Wholeness |
| 2:25 pm | Evaluation |
| 2:30 pm | Departure and Team Meeting |

### Materials
*for the retreat:*
- copies of *Quick Takes for Teens*, Volume 3, 1 per Team Leader
- Bibles
- name-tag supplies
- photocopies of Journal #11 (page 110), 1 per participant
- photocopies of the Evaluation (page 114), 1 per participant
- pens or pencils
- index cards
- snacks, rice and food scraps
- CD player
- CDs appropriate for break and reflection times
- adhesive name tags
- newsprint
- masking tape
- colored felt markers
- food and beverages for breaks and lunch

*for the ritual:*
- recorded or printed music:
  — "Blest Are They" by David Haas (GIA) or "We Are the Light of the World" by Steve Agrisano (OCP)
  — "For Living, For Dying" by Donna Peña (GIA) or "No Longer the Stranger" by Jesse Manibusan (OCP)
  — "Sing Out Gladly (Munezero)" by Leonidas Ntibimenya (GIA) or "Sing Alleluia" by Janet Vogt (OCP)

- items for donation
- large baskets

### Advance Preparation Checklist

☐ Set the date and reserve the site. Check both school and parish calendars!

☐ Read through the Retreat Plan. Decide which activities to include, substitute, adapt, etc.

☐ Recruit and train the Retreat Team. See the Introduction, page 1.

☐ Invite several members of your church's or community's social action groups to prepare a brief presentation on poverty in your community. This presentation will be made in Session 3 in the activity "Rich vs. Poor." Ask speakers to include a description of ways the social action groups are currently responding to these needs.

☐ Decide who will preside at the Closing Ritual. Ask the presider to prepare the Reflection to be given in the ritual. In the Reflection, the presider shares thoughts on the Beatitudes (Matthew 5:1-12). The following questions also may help in preparation:
  — Which beatitude most resonates with my life?
  — Which beatitude most challenges me?
  — In what ways can I help those who suffer because of social and economic injustice?

As a part of the Reflection, the presider may wish to have the assembly reflect on any one of these same questions, either silently or in groups of no more than three members each.

☐ Recruit a Team Member to give the Witness Talk in Session 2. Besides the basic guidelines given in the Introduction (page 2), suggest to the Team Member:
  — In your talk, reflect on one of these passages: Proverbs 25:21, Isaiah 58:7-10 or Ezekiel 18:5, 7.
  — Share a personal experience of hunger and plenty, of want and abundance.

☐ Recruit two volunteers to present the reading in today's Closing Ritual.

☐ Be ready to present specific "gifts" (items to be donated to a charitable cause) during the Closing Ritual:
  — First, identify a special need or social service in your parish or community for which you would like to collect donations.
  — Second, ask the identified organization to provide information about their ministry and to suggest specific items that could be donated, for example, blankets for a homeless shelter, coats for a children's abuse center or supplies to work on a Habitat for Humanity home.
  — Third, alert participants to bring these items to the Retreat to be given during the Closing Ritual.

☐ Arrange for food and beverages.

☐ Arrange for transportation, as necessary.

☐ Get permission slips, as necessary.

☐ Photocopy necessary materials, for example, Journal Sheets and Evaluations.

☐ Collect and pack materials.

☐ Envision the environment and prepare necessary materials. See the Introduction, page 2.

☐ Pre-assign participants to small groups. Assign a Team Member to facilitate each group. Determine locations for small-group discussions.

## RETREAT PLAN

**8:00 am** Team Arrives for Set-Up and Team Meeting
See the Introduction, page 2.

**9:00 am** Participants Arrive

### Name Tags
See the Introduction, page 3, or *Quick Takes for Teens*, Volume 3, page 7.

**9:15 am** Welcome
See the Introduction, pages 3-4.

### Team Introductions
(5 minutes)

### Rules
(5 minutes)

**Overview of the Day**
(5 minutes)

**9:30 am**  Session 1: Community Building

We suggest the following icebreakers. Add your favorites or choose others from *Quick Takes for Teens*, Volume 3, pages 6-7.

### Song Rewrite
(15 minutes)
See *Quick Takes for Teens*, Volume 3, page 6.

### If I Could...
(20 minutes)
See *Quick Takes for Teens*, Volume 3, page 7.

**10:15 am**  Snack Break and Team Check-In
See the Introduction, page 2.

### Food for All?
See *Quick Takes for Teens*, Volume 3, page 32.
Note that this activity *is* the break between Sessions 1 and 2.

**10:30 am**  Session 2: Hunger

### Less Means More
(15 minutes)
See *Quick Takes for Teens*, Volume 3, page 34.

### Re-act-ion
(15 minutes)
See *Quick Takes for Teens*, Volume 3, page 30.

Refocus the group's attention and introduce the Witness Talk Team Member.

### Witness Talk
(10 minutes)
See Introduction, page 2, and the Advance Preparation Checklist, above.

### Hunger is...
(20 minutes)
See *Quick Takes for Teens*, Volume 3, page 32.

**11:30 am**  Lunch and Team Check-In
See the Introduction, page 2.

**12:15 pm**  Session 3: Homelessness

### Real Homelessness
(15 minutes)
See *Quick Takes for Teens*, Volume 3, page 32.

### Rich vs. Poor
(25 minutes)
See *Quick Takes for Teens*, Volume 3, page 35.

### Journal Reflection
(15 minutes)
Distribute pens or pencils, Bibles and photocopies of Journal #11. Invite participants to work individually to complete the sheet.

After about 10 minutes, regather and invite volunteers to share their insights with the group.

### Stretch Break
(5 minutes)
Give group members a brief break while you prepare for the next session.

**1:15 pm**  Session 4: What Can I Do?

### Greed or Goodness
(20 minutes)
See *Quick Takes for Teens*, Volume 3, page 28.

### Balancing Pleasure
(25 minutes)
See *Quick Takes for Teens*, Volume 3, page 36.

# Ritual

**2:00 pm** Closing Ritual: Justice, Peace and Wholeness

**Gathering Song**
Sing together "Blest Are They" or "We Are the Light of the World."

**Introductory Rite**

*Presider:*
As we gather, we rejoice that God is with us in our poverty, offering encouragement and support, and that God challenges us to share our wealth, food and possessions with those in need.

**Scripture**
Volunteers read the following adaptation of the Beatitudes (Matthew 5:3-12). Throughout the reading, play an instrumental version of the refrain *only* of "Blest Are They" or of the refrain *only* of "We Are the Light of the World." (Thank you to Christ the King Catholic Community of Las Vegas, Nevada, for the idea for this reading.)

*Reader 1:*
Happy are those who know they are spiritually poor; the Kingdom of heaven belongs to them.

*Reader 2:*
Sure, the kingdom may belong to me, but it doesn't help when I'm lost and wandering the streets. Are any of you willing to face me and help me in my despair?

*Reader 1:*
Happy are those who mourn; God will comfort them.

*Reader 2:*
Comfort? What is that when my heart has been ripped? Will you stand before my pain and taste my tears and hold me?

*Reader 1:*
Happy are those who are humble; they will receive what God has promised.

*Reader 2:*
And what if I am humbled in front of my friends? Will you stick up for me or even know that I am present?

*All:*
(Sing together the refrain of "Blest Are They" or the refrain of "We Are the Light of the World.")

*Reader 1:*
Happy are those whose greatest desire is to do what God requires: God will satisfy them fully!

*Reader 2:*
And so I have decided to stand up for what I believe the church to be teaching about social and economical issues. Can you stand by me even if it means changing your own lifestyle?

*Reader 1:*
Happy are those who are merciful to others; God will be merciful to them.

*Reader 2:*
I look around and try to help others in need. Why aren't you helping me? I feel all alone; I need to feel your presence as we minister together. Can you take that chance?

*Reader 1:*
Happy are the pure in heart; they will see God.

*Reader 2:*
And yet because of the way I have lived my life I am not that pure.

I still want to see God, but I need your help. Open your heart—help me understand that reaching God is possible.

*All:*
> (Sing together the refrain of "Blest Are They" or the refrain of "We Are the Light of the World.")

*Reader 1:*
> Happy are those who work for peace; they will be called God's children!

*Reader 2:*
> Peace? Ha! In a world of violence? It is so easy for me to be cynical. Will you stand with me and help me overcome my desire to act with violence?

*Reader 1:*
> Happy are those who are persecuted because they do what God requires; the kingdom of heaven belongs to them.

*Reader 2:*
> Persecuted? Hurt by others? This frightens me! Sometimes I may even do the hurting and persecuting. Can you face my insecurities and help me reach out to God?

*Reader 1:*
> Happy are you when people insult you and persecute you and tell all kinds of evil lies against you because you are my followers.

*Reader 2:*
> Happiness? When I am insulted? Seems like a contradiction! But isn't that just like our world—filled with contradictions. Can you face me and love me even when I am confused?

*All:*
> (Sing together the refrain of "Blest Are They" or the refrain of "We Are the Light of the World.")

Observe a minute or two of silence.

## Reflection

The presider shares a few thoughts in response to the Beatitudes (Matthew 5:1-12). See Introduction, page 5, and the Advance Preparation Checklist, above.

## Ritual Action

The presider talks about the chosen charity, sharing information provided by the charity. Start playing the music for "For Living, For Dying" or "No Longer the Stranger." Invite participants to bring their donations to the front, placing them in the large baskets. When all the gifts have been collected, ask volunteers to carry the baskets in procession around room as you sing together "For Living, For Dying" or "No Longer the Stranger."

When the baskets have circled the room and returned to the front, the presider continues:

*Presider:*
> Having been attentive to the needs of the poor, let us stand and pray in the words Christ himself gave us:

*All:*
> Our Father... Amen.

*Presider:*
> The Lord be with you.

*All:*
> And also with you.

*Presider:*
> Let us bow our heads and pray for God's blessing:
>
> God of mercy, bless our work with the poor.

*All:*
> Amen.

*Presider:*
Christ Jesus, bless our actions of justice.

*All:*
Amen.

*Presider:*
Holy Spirit, bless our lives, making us instruments of your peace.

*All:*
Amen.

*Presider:*
And may we all be blessed, Father, Son and Holy Spirit.

*All:*
Amen.

*Presider:*
Let us go forth to love and serve our God.

*All:*
Thanks be to God!

Invite participants to exchange a Sign of Peace.

**Closing Song**
Sing together "Sing Out Gladly (Munezero)" or "Sing Alleluia."

**2:25 pm** Evaluation
See the Introduction, page 4.

**2:30 pm** Departure and Team Meeting
See the Introduction, pages 2 and 4.

# RETREAT #12:
## Overnight Model: World Problems

## GETTING READY

### Focus
Retreat #12 combines elements of Retreats #9-11 to take a broad look at a several problems that span the globe, more specifically, the power of the media, the environment, violence, AIDS, hunger and homelessness. Participants explore the scope of these issues, what guidance scripture offers and what can be done to help alleviate such problems.

### Core Questions
- In what ways are we affected by these global concerns? In what ways do we *contribute* to these problems.
- What does God have to say about the media? about the environment? about violence? about AIDS? about hunger? about homelessness?
- What can we as individuals and as the Church do to bring healing to a hurting world?

### Overview
*first day:*
| | |
|---|---|
| 6:00 pm | Team Arrives for Set-Up and Team Meeting |
| 7:00 pm | Participants Arrive |
| 7:15 pm | Welcome: Team Introductions, Rules and Overview of the Day |
| 7:30 pm | Session 1: Community Building |
| 8:30 pm | Snack Break and Team Check-In |
| 8:45 pm | Session 2: Media Mania |
| 9:45 pm | Session 3: Digging for the Truth |
| 10:30 pm | Social Time and Team Check-In |
| 11:30 pm | Compline |
| 12:00 am | Bedtime |
| 12:30 am | Lights Out |

*second day:*
| | |
|---|---|
| 8:30 am | Wake-Up |
| 9:00 am | Breakfast |
| 9:45 am | Morning Prayer |
| 10:15 am | Session 4: The Environment/Violence |
| 12:00 pm | Lunch and Team Check-In |
| 1:00 pm | Session 5: AIDS/Hunger |
| 2:30 pm | Snack Break and Team Check-In |
| 3:00 pm | Session 6: Homelessness/What Can I Do? |
| 4:30 pm | Closing Ritual |
| 5:00 pm | Departure and Team Meeting |

### Materials
*for the retreat:*
- copies of *Quick Takes for Teens*, Volume 3, 1 per Team Leader
- Bibles
- name-tag supplies
- newsprint
- colored felt markers
- masking tape
- three-hole folders, 1 per participant
- colored paper or paper with pre-printed designs
- three-hole punch
- photocopies of Journal Sheets #9 (page 108), #10 (page 109) and #11 (page 110), 1 for each per participant

- photocopies of the Evaluation (page 114), 1 per participant
- pens or pencils
- paper
- index cards
- CD player
- CDs appropriate for break and reflection times.
- video television sampler (See the Advance Preparation Checklist, below.)
- examples of entertainment options available to teenagers (See the Advance Preparation Checklist, below.)
- videotapes prepared in advance by several retreat participants (See the Advance Preparation Checklist, below.)
- video sampler of television violence (See the Advance Preparation Checklist, below.)
- TV and VCR
- printed information on AIDS (See the Advance Preparation Checklist, below.)
- 2 large sheets of poster board
- scissors
- recent magazines geared for youth and/or dealing with fashion or fitness
- glue sticks
- food and beverages for breaks and meals

*for the ritual:*
In the Advance Preparation Checklist, below, you will be asked to choose a Closing Ritual for this retreat from Retreats #9, 10 or 11. The materials you will need for that ritual will be found in the materials list for that retreat.

## Advance Preparation Checklist

- [ ] Set the date and reserve the site. Check both school and parish calendars!
- [ ] Read through the Retreat Plan. Decide which activities to include, substitute, adapt, etc.
- [ ] Recruit and train the Retreat Team. See the Introduction, page 1.
- [ ] Recruit a Team Member to give the Witness Talk in Session 6. Besides the basic guidelines given in the Introduction (page 2), suggest to the Team Member:
  — In your talk, reflect on Proverbs 28:27.
  — Share a personal experience of the disparity between poverty and wealth.
- [ ] Create Retreat Journals for each participant:
  — Photocopy Journal Sheets #9, #10, #11 and #12.
  — Alternate the Journal Sheets with sheets of blank paper.
  — Three-hole punch all sheets and bind them in three-hole folders.
  — For visual interest, use colorful paper or paper with pre-printed designs, available at office supply stores.
- [ ] Invite several participants to bring videotapes of what they consider to be entertaining television programming. Each tape should include no more than 5 minutes of materials. Ask participants *not* to bring anything potentially offensive due to language, sex or violence.
- [ ] Prepare a video sampler of 10 minutes of television: a commercial, parts of a music video, a segment of a popular sitcom or soap opera, etc.
- [ ] Collect examples or symbols of entertainment options available for teens, for example, a concert ticket stub, a novel, a CD, a teen-oriented magazine, a video game cartridge, etc.
- [ ] Prepare a video sampler of television violence. Keep segments to 30 seconds or less and include clips from a variety of shows, including the news, so-called "reality shows," sports, music videos, TV dramas and cartoons.
- [ ] Call the National AIDS Hotline at 1-800-342-AIDS and request pamphlets about AIDS written for teenagers. Or contact your local health department for current information on AIDS and AIDS prevention.
- [ ] Invite several members of a church or community social action group to prepare a brief presentation on poverty in your community. This presentation will be made in Session 3 in the activity "Rich vs. Poor." Ask speakers to include a description of ways the social action groups are currently responding to these needs.
- [ ] Choose two of the Rituals from Retreat 9 (page 56, on Advertising and the Media), Retreat 10 (page 63, on Violence, the Environment and AIDS) or Retreat 11 (page 68, on Poverty, Wealth, Hunger and Homelessness). Decide which you will use

for Morning Prayer and which for the Closing Ritual. Also decide who will preside at these rituals. Ask the presider to prepare the Reflection to be given in each ritual. Specific suggestions for these Reflections are given in the corresponding Advance Preparation Checklist in each of the three retreats.
- [ ] Arrange for food and beverages.
- [ ] Arrange for transportation, as necessary.
- [ ] Get permission slips, as necessary.
- [ ] Photocopy necessary materials, for example, Journal Sheets and Evaluations.
- [ ] Collect and pack materials.
- [ ] Envision the environment and prepare necessary materials. See page 2 of the Introduction.
- [ ] Pre-assign participants to small groups. Assign a Team Member to facilitate each group. Determine locations for small-group discussions.

## RETREAT PLAN

*first day:*

**6:00 pm**  Team Arrives for Set-Up and Team Meeting
See the Introduction, page 2.

**7:00 pm**  Participants Arrive

### Name Tags
See the Introduction, page 3, or *Quick Takes for Teens*, Volume 3, page 7.

**7:15 pm**  Welcome
See the Introduction, pages 3-4.

### Team Introductions
*(5 minutes)*

### Rules and Overview of the Day
*(5 minutes)*

### Distribution of Journals
*(5 minutes)*
Distribute pens or pencils and the Retreat Journals prepared before the retreat. Explain:
- Throughout the retreat, feel free to use the blank pages in your Retreat Journal to record your feelings, thoughts, ideas and reaction.
- Two of the Journal Sheets—#9 and #10—will be used in activities we do together.
- The remaining Journal Sheets are yours to use as you wish.
- Please put your name on the front of your folder, to help you keep track of it.

If time allows, you could invite participants to list on one of the blank pages of their Retreat Journals two or three hopes they have for the retreat. Ask volunteers to share what they have written.

**7:30 pm**  Session 1: Community Building
We suggest the following icebreakers. Add your favorites or choose others from *Quick Takes for Teens*, Volume 3, pages 6-7.

### Song Rewrite
*(15 minutes)*
See *Quick Takes for Teens*, Volume 3, page 6.

### If I Could...
*(20 minutes)*
See *Quick Takes for Teens*, Volume 3, page 7.

**8:30 pm**  Snack Break and Team Check-In
See the Introduction, page 2.

**8:45 pm**  Session 2: Media Mania

### Gluttony or Entertainment?
*(20 minutes)*
See *Quick Takes for Teens*, Volume 3, page 16.

**Journal Reflection**
*(15 minutes)*
Distribute pens or pencils and invite participants to work individually to complete Journal #9, found in their Retreat Journals.

After about 10 minutes, regather and invite volunteers to share their insights with the group.

**Television Mesmerism**
*(20 minutes)*
See *Quick Takes for Teens*, Volume 3, page 19.

**Stretch Break**
*(5 minutes)*
Give group members a brief break while you prepare for the next session.

**9:45 pm** Session 3: Digging for the Truth

**Behind the Hype**
*(15 minutes)*
See *Quick Takes for Teens*, Volume 3, page 26.

**Who Am I Supposed to Be?**
*(15 minutes)*
See *Quick Takes for Teens*, Volume 3, page 22.

**What's Normal?**
*(15 minutes)*
See *Quick Takes for Teens*, Volume 3, page 24.

**10:30 pm** Social Time and Team Check-In
See the Introduction, page 2.

**11:30 pm** Compline
See the Introduction, pages 6-7, and the Advance Preparation Checklist, above.

**12:00 am** Bedtime

**12:30 am** Lights Out

*second day:*
**8:30 am** Wake-Up

**9:00 am** Breakfast

**9:45 am** Morning Prayer
See the Introduction, pages 6-7, and the Advance Preparation Checklist, above.

**10:15 am** Session 4: The Environment/Violence

**An Environmental Thing**
*(20 minutes)*
See *Quick Takes for Teens*, Volume 3, page 9.

**God and The Environment**
*(20 minutes)*
See *Quick Takes for Teens*, Volume 3, page 10.

**Stretch Break**
*(5 minutes)*
Give group members a brief break before continuing with the session.

**Horror Snippets**
*(20 minutes)*
See *Quick Takes for Teens*, Volume 3, page 43.

**Marketing Violence**
*(20 minutes)*
See *Quick Takes for Teens*, Volume 3, page 41.

### Journal Reflection
*(20 minutes)*
Distribute pens or pencils and invite participants to work individually to complete Journal #10, found in their Retreat Journals.

After about 10 minutes, regather and invite volunteers to share their stories with the group.

**12:00 pm** Lunch and Team Check-In
See the Introduction, page 2.

**1:00 pm** Session 5: AIDS/Hunger

### AIDS Graffiti
*(10 minutes)*
See *Quick Takes for Teens,* Volume 3, page 8.

### AIDS Accounts
*(15 minutes)*
See *Quick Takes for Teens,* Volume 3, page 11.

### Aiding People with AIDS
*(20 minutes)*
See *Quick Takes for Teens,* Volume 3, page 12.

### Stretch Break
*(5 minutes)*
Give group members a brief break before continuing with the session.

### Re-act-ion
*(15 minutes)*
See *Quick Takes for Teens,* Volume 3, page 30.

### Hunger is...
*(25 minutes)*
See *Quick Takes for Teens,* Volume 3, page 32.

**2:30 pm** Snack Break and Team Check-In
See the Introduction, page 2.

**3:00 pm** Session 6: Homelessness/What Can I Do?

### Real Homelessness
*(20 minutes)*
See *Quick Takes for Teens,* Volume 3, page 32.

### Rich vs. Poor
*(20 minutes)*
See *Quick Takes for Teens,* Volume 3, page 35.

Refocus the group's attention and introduce the Witness Talk Team Member.

### Witness Talk
*(10 minutes)*
See the Introduction, page 2, and the Advance Preparation Checklist, above.

### Greed or Goodness
*(20 minutes)*
See *Quick Takes for Teens,* Volume 3, page 28.

### Balancing Pleasure
*(20 minutes)*
See *Quick Takes for Teens,* Volume 3, page 36.

**4:30 pm** Closing Ritual
See the Advance Preparation Checklist, above.

**4:55 pm** Evaluation
See the Introduction, page 4.

**5:00 pm** Departure and Team Meeting
See the Introduction, pages 2 and 4.

# CHAPTER 4

## RETREAT #13:
### PREJUDICE AND RACISM

## GETTING READY

### Focus
Retreat #13 examines prejudice and racism. Participants explore the destructive power of prejudice and racism, the sources of such attitudes and ways to overcome them, both in themselves and others.

### Core Questions
- Where do prejudice and racism come from?
- Where do we see prejudice and racism in our homes, schools and communities?
- Where do we see prejudice and racism in *ourselves*?
- What does God have to say about prejudice and racism?
- How can we work to overcome prejudice and racism in our families, schools, communities and selves?

### Overview
| | |
|---|---|
| 8:00 am | Team Arrives for Set-Up and Team Meeting |
| 9:00 am | Participants Arrive |
| 9:15 am | Welcome: Team Introductions, Rules and Overview of the Day |
| 9:30 am | Session 1: Community Building |
| 10:15 am | Snack Break and Team Check-In |
| 10:30 am | Session 2: Groups and Cliques |
| 11:30 am | Lunch and Team Check-In |
| 12:15 pm | Session 3: Understanding Others |
| 1:15 pm | Session 4: Finding Freedom |
| 2:00 pm | Closing Ritual: Letting Go of Prejudice |
| 2:25 pm | Evaluation |
| 2:30 pm | Departure and Team Meeting |

### Materials
*for the retreat:*
- copies of *Quick Takes for Teens,* Volume 4, 1 per Team Leader
- Bibles
- name-tag supplies
- sculpting media
- newsprint
- colored felt markers
- photocopies of Journal #13 (page 111), 1 per participant
- photocopies of the Evaluation (page 114), 1 per participant
- scissors
- recent newspapers and news magazines
- pens or pencils
- paper
- food and beverages for breaks and lunch
- masking tape
- matches
- fireproof container (e.g., metal bucket or trash can)
- fire extinguisher

*for the ritual:*
- recorded or printed music:
  — "If" by Rory Cooney (GIA) or "Agua Viva" by Jesse Manibusan (OCP)
  — "Hold Us in Your Mercy" by Gary Daigle and Rory Cooney (GIA) or "Kyrie" by Jesse Manibusan (OCP)
  — a musical setting of Psalm 104 that is familiar to your community

### Advance Preparation Checklist

- [ ] Set the date and reserve the site. Check both school and parish calendars!
- [ ] Read through the Retreat Plan. Decide which activities to include, substitute, adapt, etc.
- [ ] Recruit and train the Retreat Team. See page 1 of the Introduction.
- [ ] Recruit a Team Member to give the Witness Talk in Session 2. In addition to the basic guidelines given in the Introduction (page 2), suggest to the Team Member:
    — In your talk, reflect on 1 Corinthians 1:10-17.
    — Share about ways in which "divisions" in your family, school or church have caused you pain, and how you dealt with that pain.
- [ ] Decide who will preside at the Closing Ritual. Ask the presider to prepare the Reflection to be given in the ritual. In the Reflection, the presider shares thoughts on prejudice and racism. The following questions may help in preparation:
    — When and where in life have your experienced prejudice and racism?
    — In what ways have you faced your *own* prejudice? What stereotypes do you carry within? What have you done to confront and overcome them?
    — What challenge can you offer to others as they face prejudice and racism from without and unfair stereotyping from within?

    As a part of the Reflection, the presider may wish to have the assembly reflect on any one of these same questions, either silently or in groups of no more than three members each.
- [ ] Decide who will participate in the scripture reading in today's Closing Ritual. You will need five volunteers. Choose from one of these two options:
    — *Option 1:* Ask each volunteer to read Acts 2:1-6 in a different language. Begin with English (or the language most often used in your parish). After the first reader finishes verse 1 and begins verse 2, a second reader begins reading verse 1 in another language. A third reader — reading a third language — begins reading as the second reader gets to verse 2. Enjoy the wonderful, confusing blending of languages!
    — *Option 2:* Ask all five volunteers to read Acts 2:1-6 in English (or the language most often used in your parish). The first reader begins with verse 1. When the first reader gets to verse 2, the second reader begins reading at verse 1. When the second reader gets to verse 2, the third reader begins reading at verse 1. Continue with the remaining readers. Enjoy the wonderful, confusing reading of the scripture!
- [ ] Arrange for food and beverages.
- [ ] Arrange for transportation, as necessary.
- [ ] Get permission slips, as necessary.
- [ ] Photocopy necessary materials, for example, Journal Sheets and Evaluations.
- [ ] Collect and pack materials.
- [ ] Envision the environment and prepare necessary materials. See the Introduction, page 2.
- [ ] Pre-assign participants to small groups. Assign a Team Member to facilitate each group. Determine locations for small-group discussions.

## RETREAT PLAN

**8:00 am** Team Arrives for Set-Up and Team Meeting
See the Introduction, page 2.

**9:00 am** Participants Arrive

**Name Tags**
See the Introduction, page 3.

**9:15 am** Welcome
See the Introduction, pages 3-4.

**Team Introductions**
(5 minutes)

**Rules**
(5 minutes)

**Overview of the Day**
(5 minutes)

**9:30 am** Session 1: Community Building

We suggest the following icebreakers. Add your favorites or choose others from *Quick Takes for Teens*, Volume 4, pages 6-7.

### Party Games
*(20 minutes)*
See *Quick Takes for Teens*, Volume 4, page 7.

### Sculpt It
*(15 minutes)*
See *Quick Takes for Teens*, Volume 4, page 7.

**10:15 am** Snack Break and Team Check-In
See the Introduction, page 2.

**10:30 am** Session 2: Groups and Cliques

### Tons-O'-Groups
*(15 minutes)*
See *Quick Takes for Teens*, Volume 4, page 11.

### Groups: Good and Bad
*(15 minutes)*
See *Quick Takes for Teens*, Volume 4, page 13.

### Cutting Cliques
*(20 minutes)*
See *Quick Takes for Teens*, Volume 4, page 13.

### Witness Talk
*(10 minutes)*
See the Introduction, page 3, and the Advance Preparation Checklist, above.

**11:30 am** Lunch and Team Check-In
See the Introduction page 2.

**12:15 pm** Session 3: Understanding Others

### Accepting Our Differences
*(20 minutes)*
See *Quick Takes for Teens*, Volume 4, page 10.

### Step Inside (Cross the Line)
*(20 minutes)*
Begin by creating a taped circle on the floor in the center of the meeting space, large enough to hold all members of the group. Invite participants to gather, standing *outside of* the circle. Explain:
- This is a silent activity.
- I will give an instruction about who may enter the circle. If you're included, cross the line and step inside the circle.
- Once you're in the circle, get in touch with what it feels like to be included. Do you feel uncomfortable? proud? accepted? judged?
- At the same time, if you remain outside of the circle, observe how *you* feel, too.
- Remember to remain silent.
- After a few seconds, I'll ask those in the circle to step back out.

Begin with the following instructions. Let those who step into the circle remain inside it in silence for 10-15 seconds before asking them to return to their places outside of the circle. Feel free to add other instructions of your own. *Suggested instructions:*
- If you were born in the United States, step inside.
- If you were born in a country other than the United States, step inside.
- If your parents were born in the U.S., step inside.
- If your parents were born outside the U.S., step inside.
- If you are Caucasian (or African-American, Asian, Hispanic, etc.), step inside.
- If you are Christian (or Catholic, Protestant, Jewish, Hindu, Buddhist, etc.), step inside.
- If you are male (or female), step inside.
- If you are the oldest (or youngest, middle) in your family, step inside.
- If you have ever told a racist joke, step inside.
- If you have ever *laughed* at a racist joke, step inside.

- If you have ever called a person of another race a derogatory name, either to their face or behind their back, step inside.
- If you have ever felt superior because of your race, step inside.

At the conclusion of this activity, ask participants to sit quietly while you read aloud 1 Corinthians 12-31. Divide into small groups and ask groups to discuss:
- How did you feel when you were *inside* the circle?
  — When did you feel most comfortable stepping inside the circle?
  — When did you feel least comfortable?
- How did you feel when you were *outside* the circle?
  — When did you feel most comfortable remaining outside the circle?
  — When did you feel least comfortable?
- How does this activity reflect prejudice in our world?
- Reflect on Paul's letter to the Corinthians. How does Paul challenge Christians living in today's society?

### History of Prejudice
*(15 minutes)*
See *Quick Takes for Teens*, Volume 4, page 9.

### Stretch Break
*(5 minutes)*
Give group members a brief break while you prepare for the next session.

**1:15 pm** Session 4: Finding Freedom

### People Stereotypes
*(15 minutes)*
See *Quick Takes for Teens*, Volume 4, page 11.

### Journal Reflection
*(15 minutes)*
Distribute pens or pencils and photocopies of Journal #13. Invite participants to work individually to complete this sheet.

If time allows, divide participants into smaller groups of 5-7 members each. Invite groups to share their insights.

### Racism or Salvation?
*(15 minutes)*
See *Quick Takes for Teens*, Volume 4, page 12.
Regather participants and complete this final activity outdoors in the large group. **Note:** Keep the fire extinguisher close by, just in case!

## Ritual

**2:00 pm** Closing Ritual: Letting Go of Prejudice

### Gathering Song
Sign together "If" or "Agua Viva."

### Introductory Rite
*Presider:*
   In the name of the Father and of the Son and of the Holy Spirit.

*All:*
   Amen.

*Presider:*
   The Lord be with you.

*All:*
   And also with you.

*Presider:*
   We come from different homes, different neighborhoods, differing cultures, different backgrounds. Sometimes the differences divide us.

Yet we are one in Christ, and while we recognize and appreciate our differences, we open ourselves to healing the divisions they cause.

Together sing the penitential rite, either "Hold Us in Your Mercy" or "Kyrie."

## Scripture

*Presider:*
A reading from the Acts of the Apostles.

Volunteer readers read Acts 2:1-6. See the Advance Preparation Checklist, above.

*Presider:*
The word of the Lord.

*All:*
Thanks be to God.

## Psalm

Sing a setting of Psalm 104.

## Reflection

The presider shares a few thoughts on prejudice and racism. See the Introduction, page 5, and the Advance Preparation Checklist, above.

## Ritual Action

*Presider:*
As people of God, we ask for our eyes to be opened to the ways of the Lord. Let us kneel and pray:

All kneel. In the background, softly play the penitential song used earlier in the ritual.

*Presider:*
God of light, you are the source of unfailing light. Cast out the darkness of prejudice and racism. Pour forth the light of truth upon us, your human family.

Hear our prayers today. Enable us to pass from darkness to light, to be delivered from the prince of darkness, to live always as children of the light. We ask this through Christ our Lord,

*All:*
Amen.

Invite participants to stand, pair off and pray with their partners. Ask them to pray that everyone's hearts will be opened to willingly accept others, despite their differences.

## Litany of Acceptance

*Presider:*
Let us now raise our prayers to the God who calls us to be open to all people:

For all the church throughout the world, that we may join in peace and harmony regardless of race or creed, let us pray to the Lord.

*All:*
Lord, hear our prayer.

*Presider:*
For the world and all who suffer because or racial injustice, let us pray to the Lord.

*All:*
Lord, hear our prayer.

*Presider:*
For the oppressed, the homeless, those who feel out of place and those who feel as though they have no place in society, let us pray to the Lord.

*All:*
Lord, hear our prayer.

*Presider:*
> For our own community as we all struggle with facing racism and prejudice toward others, let us pray to the Lord.

*All:*
> Lord, hear our prayer.

Invite participants to state their own intentions, being as specific to their communities as possible. Follow each with:

*Presider:*
> Let us pray to the Lord.

*All:*
> Lord, hear our prayer.

### Concluding Rite

*Presider:*
> Let us now join in the words of unity that Christ has taught us:

*All:*
> Our Father... Amen.

*Presider:*
> The Lord be with you

*All:*
> And also with you.

*Presider:*
> Let us bow our heads and ask for God's blessing:

> May God bless you with openness to all of creation.

*All:*
> Amen.

*Presider:*
> May Christ walk with you as hope in a world of prejudice.

*All:*
> Amen.

*Presider:*
> May the Holy Spirit inspire you to be witnesses of the Gospel of love.

*All:*
> Amen

*Presider:*
> And may God bless us, Father, Son and Holy Spirit.

*All:*
> Amen.

*Presider:*
> Let us go forth to love and serve our God.

*All:*
> Thanks be to God.

Invite participants to exchange the Sign of Peace.

### Concluding Song
Sign together "If" or "Agua Viva."

**2:25 pm** Evaluation
See the Introduction, page 4.

**2:30 pm** Departure and Team Meeting
See the Introduction, pages 2 and 4.

# RETREAT #14:
## FRIENDSHIP SKILLS

## GETTING READY

### Focus
Retreat #14 offers ways for participants to improve their friendship skills. After first exploring the nature, benefits and challenges of friendship, participants look for ways to be better friends to those around them.

### Core Questions
- What kind of friendships do I have? What kind of friend am I?
- What makes friendships healthy and helpful? When can friendships be harmful?
- What can I do to improve my friendships?
- What does God have to say about friendship? What kind of friend is God?

### Overview
| | |
|---|---|
| 8:00 am | Team Arrives for Set-Up and Team Meeting |
| 9:00 am | Participants Arrive |
| 9:15 am | Welcome: Team Introductions, Rules and Overview of the Day |
| 9:30 am | Session 1: Community Building |
| 10:15 am | Snack Break and Team Check-In |
| 10:30 am | Session 2: Looking at Relationships |
| 11:30 am | Lunch and Team Check-In |
| 12:15 pm | Session 3: Learning Friendship |
| 1:15 pm | Session 4: Friendship in Scripture |
| 2:00 pm | Closing Ritual: Friendship |
| 2:25 pm | Evaluation |
| 2:30 pm | Departure and Team Meeting |

### Materials
*for the retreat:*
- copies of *Quick Takes for Teens*, Volume 4, 1 per Team Leader
- Bibles
- name-tag supplies
- newsprint or poster board
- colored felt markers
- photocopies of Journal #14 (page 112), 1 per participant
- photocopies of the Evaluation (page 114), 1 per participant
- pens or pencils
- index cards
- food and beverages for breaks and lunch
- stopwatch or watch with second hand

*for the ritual:*
- copies of songs:
  — "All Are Welcome" by Marty Haugen (GIA) or "Christ Be Our Light" by Bernadette Farrell (OCP)
  — a musical setting of Psalm 34 that is familiar to your community
  — "Yes, Lord" by Darryl Ducote (Damean Music, distributed in the U.S. by GIA) or "Our God Reigns" by Leonard E. Smith, Jr. (New Jerusalem Music, as recorded by Tom Booth on the CD "Tom Booth," OCP)
- taper candles, 1 per participant
- paper wax catchers, 1 per participant
- paschal candle or other large candle
- matches

### Advance Preparation Checklist

- [ ] Set the date and reserve the site. Check both school and parish calendars!
- [ ] Read through the Retreat Plan. Decide which activities to include, substitute, adapt, etc.
- [ ] Recruit and train the Retreat Team. See the Introduction, page 1
- [ ] Recruit *two* Team Members to give the Witness Talk in Session 2, one male and one female. Besides the basic guidelines given in the Introduction (page 2), suggest to the Team Members:
  — In your talk, reflect on Ecclesiastes 4:9-12.
  — Share ways in which friendships have helped you. Share ways in which you perceive that girls and guys approach friendship differently.
  — Allow time at the end of your talk to answer questions from participants.
- [ ] Decide who will preside at the Closing Ritual. Ask the presider to prepare the Reflection to be given in the ritual. In the Reflection, the presider shares thoughts on friendship. The following questions may help in preparation:
  — When in your life do you turn to friends for help?
  — In what ways has Christ been present in your friends?
  — What role does God play in your friendships?
  — What keeps you from deeper friendships with others and with Christ?

  As a part of the Reflection, the presider may wish to have the assembly reflect on any one of these same questions, either silently or in groups of no more than three members each.
- [ ] Recruit three volunteers to read the scripture in today's Closing Ritual. Assign each of these sections of Ecclesiastes 3:1-14 to a different reader:
  — verses 1-5
  — verses 6-8
  — verses 9-14
- [ ] Arrange for food and beverages.
- [ ] Arrange for transportation, as necessary.
- [ ] Get permission slips, as necessary.
- [ ] Photocopy necessary materials, for example, Journal Sheets and Evaluations.
- [ ] Collect and pack materials.
- [ ] Envision the environment and prepare necessary materials. See the Introduction, page 2.
- [ ] Copy onto newsprint or poster board the four "Listening Tools" found on page 36 of *Quick Takes for Teens*, Volume 4. These will be used in Session 3.
- [ ] Pre-assign participants to small groups. Assign a Team Member to facilitate each group. Determine locations for small-group discussions.

## RETREAT PLAN

**8:00 am**   Team Arrives for Set-Up and Team Meeting
See the Introduction, page 2.

**9:00 am**   Participants Arrive

**Name Tags**
See the Introduction, page 3.

**9:15 am**   Welcome
See the Introduction, pages 3-4.

**Team Introductions**
*(5 minutes)*

**Rules**
*(5 minutes)*

**Overview of the Day**
*(5 minutes)*

**9:30 am**   Session 1: Community Building
We suggest the following icebreakers. Add your favorites or choose others from *Quick Takes for Teens*, Volume 4, pages 6-7.

**Party Games**
*(20 minutes)*
See *Quick Takes for Teens*, Volume 4, page 7.

**Redo the Day**
*(10 minutes)*
See *Quick Takes for Teens*, Volume 4, page 7.

**10:15 am** Snack Break and Team Check-In
See the Introduction, page 2.

**10:30 am** Session 2: Looking at Relationships

**Tons 'O Relationships**
*(20 minutes)*
See *Quick Takes for Teens*, Volume 4, page 37.

**Sorting Out**
*(15 minutes)*
See *Quick Takes for Teens*, Volume 4, page 39.

Refocus participants' attention and introduce the Witness Talk Team Members.

**Witness Talk**
*(25 minutes)*
See the Introduction, page 2, and the Advance Preparation Checklist, above.

Note that this Witness Talk allows for *two* Team Members—male and female—to not only share times when friendship has helped them, but also to dialogue on ways that guys and girls perceive and handle friendships differently. Time is also allowed for group discussion.

**11:30 am** Lunch and Team Check-In
See the Introduction, page 2.

**12:15 pm** Session 3: Learning Friendship

**Getting it Wrong**
*(20 minutes)*
See *Quick Takes for Teens*, Volume 4, page 34.

**Leadership Skills**
*(35 minutes)*
See *Quick Takes for Teens*, Volume 4, page 36.

As you begin the activity, post the "Listening Tools" copied onto newsprint or poster board before the retreat in a place where they will be visible to all groups.

**Stretch Break**
*(5 minutes)*
Give group members a brief break while you prepare for the next session.

**1:15 pm** Session 4: Friendship in Scripture

**It's Time**
*(15 minutes)*
See *Quick Takes for Teens*, Volume 4, page 37.

**Joint Discovery**
*(15 minutes)*
See *Quick Takes for Teens*, Volume 4, page 35.

**Journal Reflection**
*(15 minutes)*
Distribute pens or pencils and photocopies of Journal #14. Invite group members to work individually to complete this sheet.

If time allows, invite participants to pair off and share their journal reflections with partners.

# Ritual

**2:00 pm**   Closing Ritual: Friendship

## Gathering Song
Distribute a taper candle and a wax catcher to each participant and gather around the paschal candle (or other large candle). Sing together "All Are Welcome" or "Christ Be Our Light."

## Introductory Rite
Light the candle.

*Presider:*
As we gather, we recognize that Jesus, our brother and friend, is present within each of us. We gather around the paschal candle (*or* this candle) to celebrate that Christ is our Light!

## Scripture
*Presider:*
A reading from the book of Ecclesiastes.

Volunteer readers, in order, read Ecclesiastes 3:1-14. See the Advance Preparation Checklist, above.

*Presider:*
The word of the Lord.

*All:*
Thanks be to God.

## Psalm
Sing together a setting of Psalm 34.

## Reflection
The presider shares a few thoughts on friendship. See the Introduction, page 5, and the Advance Preparation Checklist, above.

## Ritual Action
The presider invites a participant to step forward to the candle. The participant lights his or her taper from the candle, then returns to the group circle to pass the flame to another. As the participant passes the flame, he or she addresses the entire group:

- When I was *(description of a personal time of need)*, you were my friends because *(description of way in which the group or members of the group were of help)*.

Pass the flame until all candles have been lighted and all participants have had an opportunity to affirm the group.

## Litany of Friendship
*Presider:*
Recognizing that Christ is our good friend, we lift these prayers in love and goodness:

For the church and all who share the goodness of Christ's light, we pray to the Lord.

*All:*
Lord, hear our prayer.

*Presider:*
For our world and all who share the peace of Christ's light, we pray to the Lord.

*All:*
Lord, hear our prayer.

*Presider:*
For those who reach out to the less fortunate and offer them the hope of Christ's light, we pray to the Lord.

*All:*
Lord, hear our prayer.

*Presider:*
For those in our own community, who share the meaning of Christ's light with others, we pray to the Lord.

*All:*
> Lord, hear our prayer.

Invite participants to add their own intentions. Follow each with:

*All:*
> Lord, hear our prayer.

**Concluding Rite**

*Presider:*
> As one family of friends, let us join in the words Christ has given us:

*All:*
> Our Father... Amen.

*Presider:*
> The Lord be with you.

*All:*
> And also with you

*Presider:*
> Let us bow our heads and ask for God's blessing:
>
> May God, who is Creator of all, bless our friendships.

*All:*
> Amen.

*Presider:*
> May Christ, our eternal Friend, bless us as we struggle with our friends.

*All:*
> Amen.

*Presider:*
> May the Holy Spirit who endures forever bless us as we reach out and meet new friends.

*All:*
> Amen.

*Presider:*
> And may we be blessed Father, Son and Holy Spirit.

*All:*
> Amen.

*Presider:*
> Let us go forth to love and serve God and one another.

*All:*
> Thanks be to God.

Invite participants to exchange the Sign of Peace.

**Closing Song**
Sing together ""Yes, Lord" or "Our God Reigns."

**2:25 pm** Evaluation
See the Introduction, page 4.

**2:30 pm** Departure and Team Meeting
See the Introduction, pages 2 and 4.

# RELATIONSHIP ISSUES RETREATS

## RETREAT #15:
### TOUGH CHOICES

## GETTING READY

### Focus
Retreat #15 explores the pressures that young people face when it comes to making right choices on tough moral issues like drugs and alcohol, cheating and lying, violence and gossip.

### Core Questions
- What tough choices do today's teenagers face?
- How do we make decisions when faced with tough choices?
- What unique pressures come with choices around alcohol? drugs? gangs? lying? gossiping? cheating?
- What help does God offer when we are faced with tough choices?
- How can we help our friends and family members deal with tough moral choices?

### Overview
| | |
|---|---|
| 8:00 am | Team Arrives for Set-Up and Team Meeting |
| 9:00 am | Participants Arrive |
| 9:15 am | Welcome: Team Introductions, Rules and Overview of the Day |
| 9:30 am | Session 1: Community Building |
| 10:15 am | Snack Break and Team Check-In |
| 10:30 am | Session 2: Making Choices |
| 11:30 am | Lunch and Team Check-In |
| 12:15 pm | Session 3: Pick Your Pressure |
| 1:15 pm | Session 4: Coming Out on Top |
| 2:00 pm | Closing Ritual: From Darkness to Light |
| 2:30 pm | Departure and Team Meeting |

### Materials
*for the retreat:*
- copies of *Quick Takes for Teens,* Volume 4, 1 per Team Leader
- Bibles
- name-tag supplies
- newsprint
- colored felt markers
- old newspapers
- masking tape
- scissors
- photocopies of Journal #15 (page 113), 1 per participant
- photocopies of the Evaluation (page 114), 1 per participant
- pens or pencils
- paper
- bowl
- Skittles®, M&Ms® or other small candies
- slips of paper (if using Option 1 in Session 3)
- basket (if using Option 1 in Session 3)
- pad of paper (if using Option 3 in Session 3)
- familiar games, like Monopoly®, Uno®, Yahtzee®, etc. (if using Option 5 in Session 3)
- food and beverages for breaks and lunch

*for the ritual:*
- printed or recorded music:
  — "Over My Head" (traditional, African-American, GIA and OCP)
  — *optional:* "Hold Us in Your Mercy" by Rory Cooney and Gary Daigle (GIA) or "We Show Mercy" by Mark Friedman (OCP)

— a musical setting of Psalm 23 or Psalm 42 that is familiar to your community
— "Way, Truth and Life" by Gary Daigle (GIA) or "Malo! Malo! Thanks Be to God" by Jesse Manibusan (OCP)
— *optional:* quiet live or recorded music

## Advance Preparation Checklist

☐ Set the date and reserve the site. Check both school and parish calendars!

☐ Read through the Retreat Plan. Decide which activities to include, substitute, adapt, etc.

☐ Recruit and train the Retreat Team. See the Introduction, page 1.

☐ Decide who will preside at the Closing Ritual. Ask the presider to prepare the Reflection to be given in the ritual, reflecting on Ephesians 5:8-14 and sharing thoughts on tough moral choices and the pressure to make right decisions. The following questions also may help in preparation:
— When in your own life have you been awakened from darkness by the light of God?
— Who calls you to live as a "child of light"? How do you respond?
— Who in your life is asking you to help them move from darkness to light?
— What decisions or changes do you have to make in your life to become a better friend or "light of Christ"?

As a part of the Reflection, the presider may wish to have the assembly reflect on any one of these same questions, either silently or in groups of no more than three members each.

☐ If using Option 1 in Session 3, prepare the directions for the activity "Intoxication" (*Quick Takes for Teens,* Volume 4, page 19).

☐ If using Option 1 in Session 3, copy onto newsprint the five statistics listed in "Drugs and Despair" (*Quick Takes for Teens,* Volume 4, page 19). Post these where they will be visible for members of the group participating in Option 1.

☐ Arrange for food and beverages.

☐ Arrange for transportation, as necessary.

☐ Get permission slips, as necessary.

☐ Photocopy necessary materials, for example, Journal Sheets and Evaluations.

☐ Collect and pack materials.

☐ Envision the environment and prepare necessary materials. See the Introduction, page 2.

☐ Pre-assign participants to small groups. Assign a Team Member to facilitate each group. Determine locations for small-group discussions.

# RETREAT PLAN

**8:00 am** Team Arrives for Set-Up and Team Meeting
See the Introduction, page 2.

**9:00 am** Participants Arrive

### Name Tags
See the Introduction, page 3.

**9:15 am** Welcome
See the Introduction, pages 3-4.

### Team Introductions
*(5 minutes)*

### Rules
*(5 minutes)*

### Overview of the Day
*(5 minutes)*

**9:30 am** Session 1: Community Building
We suggest the following icebreakers. Add your favorites or choose others from *Quick Takes for Teens,* Volume 4, pages 6-7.

### Dress 'Em Up
*(20 minutes)*
See *Quick Takes for Teens,* Volume 4, page 6.

**Finding God**
*(15 minutes)*
See *Quick Takes for Teens*, Volume 4, page 7.

**10:15 am** Snack Break and Team Check-In
See the Introduction, page 2.

**10:30 am** Session 2: Making Choices

**Where to Go?**
*(20 minutes)*
See *Quick Takes for Teens*, Volume 4, page 26.

**Making Choices**
*(20 minutes)*
See *Quick Takes for Teens*, Volume 4, page 23.

**Drugs: Hooked**
*(20 minutes)*
See *Quick Takes for Teens*, Volume 4, page 20.
At the conclusion of the activity, explain:
- We can be "addicted to" more than just a substance, like alcohol or drugs.
- We can also form an "addiction to"—in the sense of unhealthy reliance upon—behaviors like violence, lying, cheating, gossip, etc.
- In Session 3, we will explore the addictive nature of several of these, and how they affect our relationships with family, friends, God and ourselves.

**11:30 am** Lunch and Team Check-In
See the Introduction, page 2.

**12:15 pm** Session 3: Pick Your Pressure
For Session 3, choose from the options offered below. Base your decision on which issues are of immediate concern to group members. You could, as a group, explore just one of these options, or divide into smaller groups and allow members to choose which area they would like to explore, using the suggested activities.

*Option 1: Drugs and Alcohol*

**Intoxication**
*(30 minutes)*
See *Quick Takes for Teens*, Volume 4, page 19.

**Drugs: Hooked**
*(30 minutes)*
See *Quick Takes for Teens*, Volume 4, page 20.

*Option 2: Gang Violence*

**Bang! You're Dead**
*(5 minutes)*
See *Quick Takes for Teens*, Volume 4, page 24.

Spend 5 minutes explaining this activity to group members. The activity itself continues throughout the following two activities.

**Plus and Minus**
*(20 minutes)*
See *Quick Takes for Teens*, Volume 4, page 24.

**Gang Folly**
*(20 minutes)*
See *Quick Takes for Teens*, Volume 4, page 24.

**Bang! You're Dead Revisited**
*(15 minutes)*
Conclude this session by inviting those group members who were "killed" to rejoin the group and share their observations and insights. Conclude the session by asking:
- What new insights do you now have about gang violence? about making gang-related choices?

*Options 3: Gossip*

**The Gossip Trap**
*(15 minutes)*
See *Quick Takes for Teens*, Volume 4, page 28.

### Why Gossip
*(15 minutes)*
See *Quick Takes for Teens*, Volume 4, page 31.

### Gossip Halt
*(30 minutes)*
See *Quick Takes for Teens*, Volume 4, page 28.

*Option 4: Lying*

### Lying Around
*(20 minutes)*
See *Quick Takes for Teens*, Volume 4, page 29.

### I Never Lie!
*(20 minutes)*
See *Quick Takes for Teens*, Volume 4, page 29.

### Truth or Consequences
*(20 minutes)*
See *Quick Takes for Teens*, Volume 4, page 32.

*Option 5: Cheating*

### Cheaters Anonymous
*(30 minutes)*
See *Quick Takes for Teens*, Volume 4, page 32.

### But Honestly
*(15 minutes)*
See *Quick Takes for Teens*, Volume 4, page 31.

### Journal Reflection
*(15 minutes)*
Distribute Bibles, pens or pencils and photocopies of Journal #15. Invite group members to work individually to complete this sheet.

After about 10 minutes, divide participants into smaller groups of 7-9 members each. Invite small groups to share their journal reflections with each other.

**1:15 pm** Session 4: Coming Out on Top
Regather the large group.

### Reality Check
*(15 minutes)*
See *Quick Takes for Teens*, Volume 4, page 22.
As you introduce and explain this activity to participants, adapt it to include all of the behaviors explored earlier in the session, for example, when asking the first question, you could rephrase it to say:

■ If you were hooked *on cheating, lying, gang involvement, etc.*, what would you need (or want) to hear from a friend?

### The Future You
*(20 minutes)*
Distribute paper and pens or pencils. Invite participants to choose one of today's "problems" to explore further in this activity. Explain:

■ Let's say you choose as your topic *cheating*. First, write the word *cheating* at the top of your paper.
■ Now think about it and project yourself into the future. You're a regular cheater. Ten years pass... Twenty years pass... How old are you now?
■ I'll pause after each of the following questions so you can write your answers on your paper. Remember to adapt the question for the topic you wrote at the top of your page:
— Knowing what your chosen "problem" can do to you, describe yourself 20 years from now. *(Pause.)*
— What has your "problem" cost you? *(Pause.)*
— How are you doing physically? mentally? emotionally? spiritually? *(Pause.)*
— How has your "problem" affected the people you know and care about? *(Pause.)*
— What kind of job—if any—have you managed to keep? *(Pause.)*

— What do the *next* 10 years of your life look like? *(Pause.)*

When group members have finished, invite volunteers to share their reflections with the group.

### A Better Future
*(10 minutes)*
Ask group members to stand in a circle. Explain:
- Imagine your future *free of* the "problem" you identified in the previous activity. It stretches before you...20, 30, 40, 50 or more years. Imagine yourself at 50, strong, healthy, satisfied, enjoying life.
- What are you doing at 50 that you still love to do and do really well?

Invite each participant to give one brief answer to this question. Examples could include: running five miles a day, singing in a rock group, traveling around the world with the money I *haven't* spent on drugs, etc.

# Ritual

**2:00 pm** Closing Ritual: From Darkness to Light

### Gathering Song
Sing together "Over My Head."

### Introductory Rite
*Presider:*
In the name of the Father, Son and Holy Spirit.

*All:*
Amen.

*Presider:*
The Lord be with you

*All:*
And also with you.

*Presider:*
As we gather, we face our God, who knows us better than all others.

As an alternative to the following, you might instead sing together "Hold Us In Your Mercy" or "We Show Mercy."

*Presider:*
Lord Jesus, you are light to those of us who live as children of darkness. Lord, have mercy...

*All:*
Lord, have mercy.

*Presider:*
Christ Jesus, you call us to ways that are pleasing to God and not our own ways. Christ, have mercy...

*All:*
Christ, have mercy.

*Presider:*
Lord Jesus, you show us how all that is dark can be light. Lord, have mercy...

*All:*
Lord, have mercy.

*Presider:*
May almighty God have mercy on us, forgive us our sins and bring us to everlasting life.

*All:*
Amen.

**Scripture**

*Reader:*
A reading from the letter to the Ephesians.

Read Ephesians 5:8-14.

*Reader:*
The word of the Lord.

*All:*
Thanks be to God.

**Psalm**
Sing a setting of Psalm 23 or Psalm 42.

**Reflection**
Presider shares a few thoughts on tough moral choices and the pressure to make right decisions. See the Introduction, page 5, and the Advance Preparation Checklist, above.

**Ritual Action**
*Presider:*
I invite you to turn to one or two other people near you and to talk honestly about your struggle to make right choices. Take this time as a friend to truly listen and to also—as appropriate—touch arms, shoulders or hands, letting the person talking know that his or her story does *not* shatter your friendship.

Allow several minutes for sharing, then continue with the Litany of Knowing.

**Litany of Knowing**
*Presider:*
During this litany, I invite us to name, in general terms, some of the ways that we are kept in darkness—big ways like alcoholism, eating disorders or violence, or simple ways like pride, fear of rejection or anger. Simply name these, one at a time. If you mention something shared privately by someone earlier in the ritual, honor their confidence by talking in broad terms; do not divulge any secrets. We will listen in silence. And remember, even though some things may not be spoken aloud, God hears them within our hearts.

Encourage responses by mentioning several ways that you, the presider, see us kept in darkness.

After all who wish to share have done so, Team Members circle the group, pausing to pray silently with each person. As they pray, they are encouraged to touch each person's shoulder or hands. You might also invite those standing nearby also to touch the person as the Team Member prays with him or her.

Maintain silence throughout this part of the ritual. Quiet instrumental music, either live or recorded, would be appropriate in the background.

**Concluding Rite**
*Presider:*
Confident that God hears us and will lift us to light, let us pray in the words Christ himself has given us:

*All:*
Our Father… Amen.

*Presider:*
The Lord be with you.

*All:*
And also with you.

*Presider:*
Let us bow our heads and ask for God's blessing:

May God bless us as we try to live by the light of life.

*All:*
Amen.

*Presider:*
May Christ bless us as we try to live by the values spoken in the gospel.

*All:*
Amen.

*Presider:*
May the Holy Spirit bless us as we try to live by the belief that we can bring the light of God's love to all.

*All:*
Amen.

*Presider:*
And may we be blessed, Father, Son and Holy Spirit.

*All:*
Amen.

*Presider:*
Our celebration has ended, but let us go forth to love and serve our God and each other.

Invite participants to exchange the Sign of Peace.

**Closing Song**
Sing together "Way, Truth and Life" or "Malo! Malo! Thanks Be to God."

**2:25 pm** Evaluation
See the Introduction, page 4.

**2:30 pm** Departure and Team Meeting
See the Introduction, pages 2 and 4.

# RETREAT #16:
## OVERNIGHT MODEL: RELATIONSHIP ISSUES

## GETTING READY

### Focus
Retreat #16 blends elements of Retreats #13-15 to take a broad look at a variety of key questions brought up in teens' relationships to each other and to the world, including friendships and cliques, prejudice and racism, and a variety of tough moral choices. Participants also practice a few helpful relationship skills.

### Core Questions
- What is the nature of friendship?
- How healthy are our friendships?
- What can we do to help friendships deepen and grow?
- Where do prejudice and racism come from?
- Where do we see prejudice and racism in our homes, schools, communities and selves?
- What can we do to overcome racism?
- What tough choices do we face in relationships?
- How can we help our friends, our families and ourselves make the right choices?

### Overview
*first day:*
| | |
|---|---|
| 6:00 pm | Team Arrives for Set-Up and Team Meeting |
| 7:00 pm | Participants Arrive |
| 7:15 pm | Welcome: Team Introductions, Rules and Overview of the Day |
| 7:30 pm | Session 1: Community Building |
| 8:30 pm | Snack Break and Team Check-In |
| 8:45 pm | Session 2: Groups and Cliques |
| 9:45 pm | Session 3: Friendship in Scripture |
| 10:30 pm | Social Time and Team Check-In |
| 11:30 pm | Compline |
| 12:00 am | Bedtime |
| 12:30 am | Lights Out |

*second day:*
| | |
|---|---|
| 8:30 am | Wake-Up |
| 9:00 am | Breakfast |
| 9:45 am | Morning Prayer |
| 10:15 am | Session 4: Prejudice and Racism |
| 12:00 pm | Lunch and Team Check-In |
| 1:00 pm | Session 5: What Are Our Choices? |
| 2:30 pm | Snack Break and Team Check-In |
| 3:00 pm | Session 6: Relationship Tool Box |
| 4:30 pm | Closing Ritual |
| 4:45 pm | Evaluation |
| 5:00 pm | Departure and Team Meeting |

### Materials
*for the retreat:*
- copies of *Quick Takes for Teens,* Volume 4, 1 per Team Leader
- Bibles
- name-tag supplies
- masking tape
- scissors
- newsprint
- colored felt markers
- photocopies of the Evaluation (page 114), 1 per participant
- CD player

- CDs appropriate for break and reflection times
- pens or pencils
- paper
- three-hole folders, 1 per participant
- colored paper or paper with pre-printed designs
- three-hole punch
- photocopies of Journal Sheets #13 (page 111), #14 (page 112) and #15 (page 113), 1 for each per participant
- food and beverages for breaks and meals

*for the ritual:*
In the Advance Preparation Checklist, below, you will be asked to choose a Closing Ritual for this retreat from Retreats #13, 14 or 15. The materials you will need for that ritual will be found in the materials list for that retreat.

## Advance Preparation Checklist

- [ ] Set the date and reserve the site. Check both school and parish calendars!
- [ ] Read through the Retreat Plan. Decide which activities to include, substitute, adapt, etc.
- [ ] Recruit and train the Retreat Team. See the Introduction, page 1.
- [ ] Recruit a Team Member to give the Witness Talk in Session 2. Besides the basic guidelines given in the Introduction (page 2), suggest to the Team Member:
  — In your talk, reflect on 1 Corinthians 1:10-17.
  — Share about ways in which "divisions" in your family, school or church have caused you pain, and how you dealt with that pain.
- [ ] If using Option 1 in Session 5, prepare the directions for the activity "Intoxication" (*Quick Takes for Teens*, Volume 4, page 19).
- [ ] If using Option 1 in Session 5, copy onto newsprint the five statistics listed in "Drugs and Despair" (*Quick Takes for Teens*, Volume 4, page 19). Post these where they will be visible for members of the group participating in Option 1.
- [ ] Choose the Ritual you think is most appropriate from Retreat 13 (page 79, on Prejudice and Racism), Retreat 14 (page 85, on Friendship Skills) or Retreat 15 (page 91, on Tough Choices). Decide who will preside at the Closing Ritual. Ask the presider to prepare the Reflection to be given in the ritual. Specific suggestions for these Reflections are given in the corresponding Advance Preparation Checklist in each of the three retreats.
- [ ] Create Retreat Journals for each participant:
  — Photocopy Journal Sheets #13, #14, and #15.
  — Alternate the Journal Sheets with sheets of blank paper.
  — Three-hole punch all sheets and bind them in three-hole folders.
  — For visual interest, use colorful paper or paper with pre-printed designs, available at office supply stores.
- [ ] Arrange for food and beverages.
- [ ] Arrange for transportation, as necessary.
- [ ] Get permission slips, as necessary.
- [ ] Photocopy necessary materials, for example, Journal Sheets and Evaluations.
- [ ] Collect and pack materials.
- [ ] Envision the environment and prepare necessary materials. See the Introduction, page 2.
- [ ] Pre-assign participants to small groups. Assign a Team Member to facilitate each group. Determine locations for small-group discussions.

## RETREAT PLAN

*first day:*

**6:00 pm**  Team Arrives for Set-Up and Team Meeting
See the Introduction, page 2.

**7:00 pm**  Participants Arrive

**Name Tags**
See the Introduction, page 3.

**7:15 pm**  Welcome
See the Introduction, pages 3-4.

**Team Introductions**
*(5 minutes)*

**Rules and Overview of the Day**
*(5 minutes)*

**Distribution of Journals**
*(5 minutes)*
Distribute pens or pencils and the Retreat Journals prepared before the retreat. Explain:
- Throughout the retreat, feel free to use the blank pages in your Retreat Journal to record your feelings, thoughts, ideas and reaction.
- One of the Journal Sheets—#15—will be used in an activity we will do together.
- The remaining two Journal Sheets—#13 and #14—are yours to use as you wish.
- Please put your name on the front of your folder, to help you keep track of it.

If time allows, you could invite participants to list on one of the blank pages of their Retreat Journals two or three hopes they have for the retreat. Ask volunteers to share what they have written.

**7:30 pm** Session 1: Community Building
We suggest the following icebreakers. Add your favorites or choose others from *Quick Takes for Teens*, Volume 4, pages 6-7.

**Dress 'Em Up**
*(20 minutes)*
See *Quick Takes for Teens*, Volume 4, page 6.

**Party Games**
*(20 minutes)*
See *Quick Takes for Teens*, Volume 4, page 7.

**8:30 pm** Snack Break and Team Check-In
See the Introduction, page 2.

**8:45 pm** Session 2: Groups and Cliques

**Getting It Wrong!**
*(15 minutes)*
See *Quick Takes for Teens*, Volume 4, page 34.

**Tons 'O Relationships**
*(15 minutes)*
See *Quick Takes for Teens*, Volume 4, page 37.

**Sorting Out**
*(15 minutes)*
See *Quick Takes for Teens*, Volume 4, page 39.

**Witness Talk**
*(10 minutes)*
See the Introduction, page 2, and the Advance Preparation Checklist, above.

**Stretch Break**
*(5 minutes)*
Give group members a brief break while you prepare for the next session.

**9:45 pm** Session 3: Friendship in Scripture

**It's Time**
*(25 minutes)*
See *Quick Takes for Teens*, Volume 4, page 37.

**Joint Discovery**
*(20 minutes)*
See *Quick Takes for Teens*, Volume 4, page 35.

**10:30 pm** Social Time and Team Check-In
See the Introduction, page 2.

**11:30 pm** Compline
See the Introduction, pages 6-7, and the Advance Preparation Checklist, above.

**12:00 am** Bedtime

**12:30 am** Lights Out

*second day:*
**8:30 am** Wake-Up

**9:00 am** Breakfast

**9:45 am** Morning Prayer
See the Advance Preparation Checklist, above.

### Seeing Inside
*(15 minutes)*
See *Quick Takes for Teens*, Volume 4, page 14.

### Someone Else's Skin
*(15 minutes)*
See *Quick Takes for Teens*, Volume 4, page 15.

As participants read aloud their prayers at the conclusion of this activity, invite the group to respond after each prayer with:
- Lord, hear our prayer.

**10:15 am** Session 4: Prejudice and Racism

### Tons-O'-Groups
*(15 minutes)*
See *Quick Takes for Teens*, Volume 4, page 11.

### Groups: Good and Bad
*(15 minutes)*
See *Quick Takes for Teens*, Volume 4, page 13.

### Cutting Cliques
*(15 minutes)*
See *Quick Takes for Teens*, Volume 4, page 13.

### Stretch Break
*(5 minutes)*
Give group members a brief break while you prepare for the next session.

### Accepting Our Differences
*(20 minutes)*
See *Quick Takes for Teens*, Volume 4, page 10.

### Step Inside (Cross the Line)
*(15 minutes)*
Begin by creating a taped circle on the floor in the center of the meeting space, large enough to hold all members of the group. Invite participants to gather, standing *outside of* the circle. Explain:
- This is a silent activity.
- I will give an instruction about who may enter the circle. If you're included, cross the line and step inside the circle.
- Once you're in the circle, get in touch with what it feels like to be included. Do you feel uncomfortable? proud? accepted? judged?
- At the same time, if you remain outside of the circle, observe how *you* feel, too.
- Remember to remain silent.
- After a few seconds, I'll ask those in the circle to step back out.

Begin with the following instructions. Let those who step into the circle remain inside it in silence for 10-15 seconds before asking them to return to their places outside of the circle. Feel free to add other instructions of your own. *Suggested instructions:*
- If you were born in the United States, step inside.
- If you were born in a country other than the United States, step inside.
- If your parents were born in the U.S., step inside.
- If your parents were born outside the U.S., step inside.
- If you are Caucasian (or African-American, Asian, Hispanic, etc.), step inside.
- If you are Christian (or Catholic, Protestant, Jewish, Hindu, Buddhist, etc.), step inside.
- If you are male (female), step inside.
- If you are the oldest (or youngest, middle) in your family, step inside.

**97**

- If you have ever told a racist joke, step inside.
- If you have ever *laughed* at a racist joke, step inside.
- If you have ever called a person of another race a derogatory name, either to their face or behind their back, step inside.
- If you have ever felt superior because of your race, step inside.

At the conclusion of this activity, ask participants to sit quietly while you read aloud 1 Corinthians 12-31. Divide into small groups and ask groups to discuss:
- How did you feel when you were *inside* the circle?
  — When did you feel most comfortable stepping inside the circle?
  — When did you feel least comfortable?
- How did you feel when you were *outside* the circle?
  — When did you feel most comfortable remaining outside the circle?
  — When did you feel least comfortable?
- How does this activity reflect prejudice in our world?
- Reflect on Paul's letter to the Corinthians. How does Paul challenge Christians living in today's society?

### History of Prejudice
*(20 minutes)*
See *Quick Takes for Teens*, Volume 4, page 9.

**12:00 pm** Lunch and Team Check-In
See the Introduction, page 2.

**1:00 pm** Session 5: What Are Our Choices?

### Drugs: Hooked
*(10 minutes)*
See *Quick Takes for Teens*, Volume 4, page 20.
At the conclusion of the activity, explain:
- We can be "addicted to" more than just a substance, like alcohol or drugs.
- We can also form an "addiction to" — in the sense of unhealthy reliance upon — behaviors like violence, lying, cheating, gossip, etc.
- Let's explore the addictive nature of several of these, and how they affect our relationships with family, friends, God and ourselves.

For the next 35 minutes of Session 5, choose from the options offered below. Base your decision on which issues are of immediate concern to group members. You could, as a group, explore just one of these options, or divide into smaller groups and allow members to choose which area they would like to explore, using the suggested activities.

*Option 1: Drugs and Alcohol*

### Intoxication
*(20 minutes)*
See *Quick Takes for Teens*, Volume 4, page 19.

### Drugs: Hooked
*(15 minutes)*
See *Quick Takes for Teens*, Volume 4, page 20.

*Option 2: Gang Violence*

### Bang! You're Dead
*(5 minutes)*
See *Quick Takes for Teens*, Volume 4, page 24.
Spend 5 minutes explaining this activity to group members. The activity itself continues throughout the following two activities.

### Plus and Minus
*(10 minutes)*
See *Quick Takes for Teens*, Volume 4, page 24.

### Gang Folly
*(15 minutes)*
See *Quick Takes for Teens*, Volume 4, page 24.

### Bang! You're Dead Revisited
*(5 minutes)*
Conclude this session by inviting those group members who were "killed" to rejoin the group and share their observations and insights. Conclude the session by asking:
- What new insights do you now have about gang violence? about making gang-related choices?

*Options 3: Gossip*

### The Gossip Trap
*(10 minutes)*
See *Quick Takes for Teens*, Volume 4, page 28.

### Why Gossip
*(10 minutes)*
See *Quick Takes for Teens*, Volume 4, page 31.

### Gossip Halt
*(15 minutes)*
See *Quick Takes for Teens*, Volume 4, page 28.

*Option 4: Lying*

### Lying Around
*(10 minutes)*
See *Quick Takes for Teens*, Volume 4, page 29.

### I Never Lie!
*(10 minutes)*
See *Quick Takes for Teens*, Volume 4, page 29.

### Truth or Consequences
*(15 minutes)*
See *Quick Takes for Teens*, Volume 4, page 32.

*Option 5: Cheating*

### Cheaters Anonymous
*(20 minutes)*
See *Quick Takes for Teens*, Volume 4, page 32.

### But Honestly
*(15 minutes)*
See *Quick Takes for Teens*, Volume 4, page 31.

*For all participants:*

### Stretch Break
*(5 minutes)*
Give group members a brief break while you prepare for the next activity.

### Journal Reflection
*(15 minutes)*
Distribute Bibles and pens or pencils and invite participants to work individually to complete Journal #15, found in their Retreat Journals.

After about 10 minutes, regather and invite volunteers to share their insights with the group.

### Where to Go?
*(10 minutes)*
See *Quick Takes for Teens*, Volume 4, page 26.

### The Future You
*(10 minutes)*
Distribute paper and pens or pencils. Invite participants to choose one of today's "problems" to explore further in this activity.
Explain:
- Let's say you choose as your topic *cheating*. First, write the word *cheating* at the top of your paper.
- Now think about it and project yourself into the future. You're a regular cheater. Ten years pass... Twenty years pass... How old are you now?

- I'll pause after each of the following questions so you can write your answers on your paper. Remember to adapt the question for the topic you wrote at the top of your page:
  — Knowing what your chosen "problem" can do to you, describe yourself 20 years from now. *(Pause.)*
  — What has your "problem" cost you? *(Pause.)*
  — How are you doing physically? mentally? emotionally? spiritually? *(Pause.)*
  — How has your "problem" affected the people you know and care about? *(Pause.)*
  — What kind of job—if any—have you managed to keep? *(Pause.)*
  — What do the *next* 10 years of your life look like? *(Pause.)*

When group members have finished, invite volunteers to share their reflections with the group.

**A Better Future**
*(5 minutes)*
Ask group members to stand in a circle. Explain:
- Imagine your future *free of* the "problem" you identified in the previous activity. It stretches before you...20, 30, 40, 50 or more years. Imagine yourself at 50, strong, healthy, satisfied, enjoying life.
- What are you doing at 50 that you still love to do and do really well?

Invite each participant to give one brief answer to this question. Examples could include: running five miles a day, singing in a rock group, traveling around the world with the money I *haven't* spent on drugs, etc.

**2:30 pm**   Snack and Team Check-In
See the Introduction, page 2.

**3:00 pm**   Session 6: Relationship Tool Box

**Leadership Skills**
*(25 minutes)*
See *Quick Takes for Teens*, Volume 4, page 36.

**Reality Check**
*(20 minutes)*
See *Quick Takes for Teens*, Volume 4, page 22.
As you introduce and explain this activity to participants, adapt it to include all of the behaviors explored earlier in the session, for example, when asking the first question, you could rephrase it to say:
- If you were hooked *on cheating, lying, gang involvement, etc.*, what would you need (or want) to hear from a friend?

**Lending Support**
*(25 minutes)*
See *Quick Takes for Teens*, Volume 4, page 38.

**Challenging**
*(20 minutes)*
See *Quick Takes for Teens*, Volume 4, page 38.

**4:30 pm**   Closing Ritual
See the Advance Preparation Checklist, above.

**4:55 pm**   Evaluation
See the Introduction, page 4.

**5:00 pm**   Departure and Team Meeting
See the Introduction, pages 2 and 4.

# FAMILY ISSUES

## JOURNAL #1
### CONFLICT IN THE FAMILY: FROM LOSE/LOSE TO WIN/WIN

Think of a recent conflict in you life, either at home, at school, with friends, wherever. Spend a few minutes writing about:
- Who was involved…

- What happened…

- What you heard other people say…

- What you heard yourself say…

- How you felt…

- What you like about how you dealt with the conflict…

- What you wish you would have done differently…

Conflict and the Word:
- Read Colossians 33:8-11. In your ~~family,~~ life, how can you "get rid of" anger, hateful feelings, insults, etc?


- Read Colossians 3:12-17. In your ~~family,~~ life, how can you "clothe yourself" with compassion, humility, patience, tolerance, forgiveness, love, peace, wisdom, etc?


Prayer Starter:
- God of Peace, just for today, help me to be a peace-maker in my family in these ways…

*Quick Takes Rituals and Retreats* © 1999 by Jean E. Bross, Robert W. Piercy and Dirk deVries. All rights reserved.
Living the Good News, a division of The Morehouse Group. 600 Grant Street, Suite 400, Denver, CO 80203. In U.S. or Canada, call 1-800-824-1813 toll free.

# FAMILY ISSUES

## JOURNAL #2
### UNDERSTANDING PARENTS

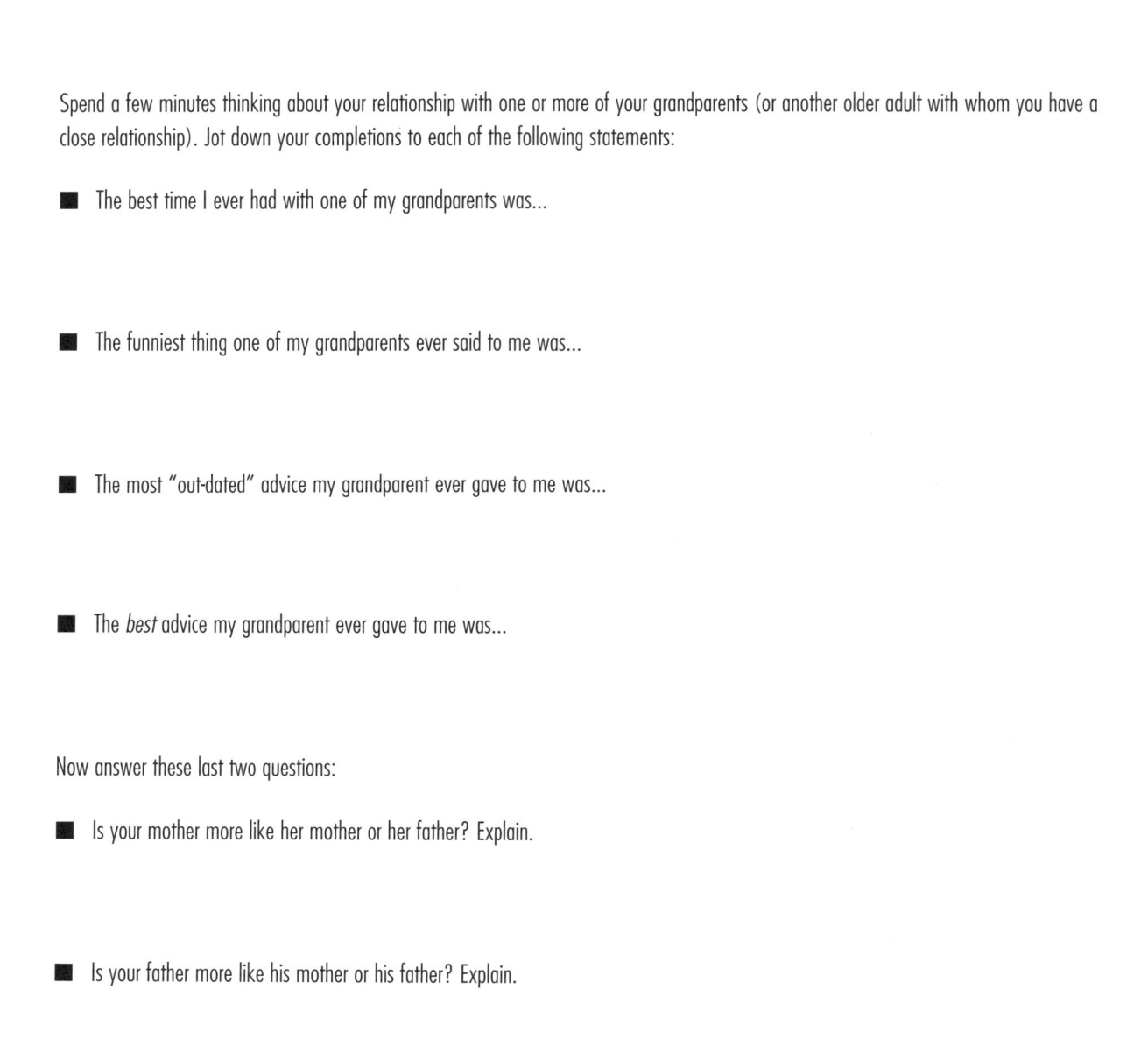

Spend a few minutes thinking about your relationship with one or more of your grandparents (or another older adult with whom you have a close relationship). Jot down your completions to each of the following statements:

■ The best time I ever had with one of my grandparents was...

■ The funniest thing one of my grandparents ever said to me was...

■ The most "out-dated" advice my grandparent ever gave to me was...

■ The *best* advice my grandparent ever gave to me was...

Now answer these last two questions:

■ Is your mother more like her mother or her father? Explain.

■ Is your father more like his mother or his father? Explain.

*Quick Takes Rituals and Retreats* © 1999 by Jean E. Bross, Robert W. Piercy and Dirk deVries. All rights reserved.
Living the Good News, a division of The Morehouse Group. 600 Grant Street, Suite 400, Denver, CO 80203. In U.S. or Canada, call 1-800-824-1813 toll free.

# FAMILY ISSUES

## JOURNAL #3
### SURVIVING SIBLINGS

You just heard a version of Jesus' Prodigal Story from Luke 15:11-32. Spend a few minutes thinking about and jotting down your answers to these questions:

■ With whom in this story did you most identify? Why?

■ Describe the personality of the younger child, including both good points and not-so-good points. How does the parent feel about this child? Who in your family is most like this child?

■ Describe the personality of the older child, including his good points and his not-so-good points. How does the parent feel about this child? Who in your family is most like this child?

■ What conflict do the two children have? How does the parent handle the conflict? In what ways are your sibling conflicts similar to the one in Jesus' story? In what ways are your solutions similar?

*Quick Takes Rituals and Retreats* © 1999 by Jean E. Bross, Robert W. Piercy and Dirk deVries. All rights reserved.
Living the Good News, a division of The Morehouse Group. 600 Grant Street, Suite 400, Denver, CO 80203. In U.S. or Canada, call 1-800-824-1813 toll free.

# TOUGH EMOTIONS

## JOURNAL #5
### BROOM TREES AND BUMMING OUT

Find 1 Kings 19:1-18 in your Bibles. Start by reading verses 1-4. Then think about the following:
- How is Elijah feeling?
- What reasons does Elijah have to feel so down?
- When in *your* life have you felt like everyone was after you? Write your answer to this question here:

Now read verses 5-10. Think about the following:
- What does God do for Elijah?
- *Now* how does Elijah feel?
- What's happened in *your* life when people have tried to help you out of your depression? Write your answer to this question here:

Now read verses 11-14.
- What do you think Elijah is meant to learn when he's nearly swept away in the wind? buried in the earthquake? burned by fire?
- What does God's soft whisper mean to Elijah?

Finally, finish the story by reading verses 15-18.
- Of what does God remind Elijah? What promises does God make about Israel's future?
- Of what do *you* need to be reminded when you feel depressed? How do *you* hear God's "whisper"? Write your answer to this question here:

*Quick Takes Rituals and Retreats* © 1999 by Jean E. Bross, Robert W. Piercy and Dirk deVries. All rights reserved.
Living the Good News, a division of The Morehouse Group. 600 Grant Street, Suite 400, Denver, CO 80203. In U.S. or Canada, call 1-800-824-1813 toll free.

# TOUGH EMOTIONS

## JOURNAL #6
### BEFORE THE DAY ENDS

Read Ephesians 4:26 in your Bible.
Write your answers to the following questions in the spaces provided:

1 With whom do you feel angry right now?

2 What can you do, before you go do bed tonight, to express your anger honestly and lovingly to the people with whom you feel angry?

3 What can you do, before you go to bed tonight, to get over some of your anger?

*Quick Takes Rituals and Retreats* © 1999 by Jean E. Bross, Robert W. Piercy and Dirk deVries. All rights reserved.
Living the Good News, a division of The Morehouse Group. 600 Grant Street, Suite 400, Denver, CO 80203. In U.S. or Canada, call 1-800-824-1813 toll free.

# TOUGH EMOTIONS

## JOURNAL #7
### LETTER TO MYSELF

In the space below, write a letter to yourself. Specifically address any areas where your self-esteem my be low.

When you've finished your letter, address your envelope to yourself. Don't put your letter in the envelope yet; volunteers will be asked to share their letters with the group.

*caring*

*gifted*

*cared for*

*great*

*capable*

*positive*

*loving*

*talented*

*Quick Takes Rituals and Retreats* © 1999 by Jean E. Bross, Robert W. Piercy and Dirk deVries. All rights reserved.
Living the Good News, a division of The Morehouse Group. 600 Grant Street, Suite 400, Denver, CO 80203. In U.S. or Canada, call 1-800-824-1813 toll free.

# TOUGH EMOTIONS

## JOURNAL #8
**GRRRRR!**

Think of a situation—either current or in the past—about which you still feel angry. In a few words, describe that situation.

*hurt*  *insult*  *injury*  *slam*

Anger often comes from fear, from the feeling that something we value is going to be taken away from us, perhaps someone we love, something we own or something we believe about ourselves, others or the world. With that in mind, ask yourself: *Why was I angry?*

*argue*  *cuss*  *ouch*

Anger itself is not bad, it's an emotion that alerts us to something important happening inside of us, something to look at and try to understand. What we *do* with our anger, however, can be good or bad. In the situation you described above, how did you handle your anger? How well (or poorly) did you think you handled your anger?

*spite*  *yell*  *revenge*

*Quick Takes Rituals and Retreats* © 1999 by Jean E. Bross, Robert W. Piercy and Dirk deVries. All rights reserved.
Living the Good News, a division of The Morehouse Group. 600 Grant Street, Suite 400, Denver, CO 80203. In U.S. or Canada, call 1-800-824-1813 toll free.

# WORLD PROBLEMS

## JOURNAL #9
### WHAT'S YOUR OPINION?

Respond in writing to at least three of these statements about modern media.

1 Movies, music videos, video games, television and the Internet encourage disrespect, violence and immorality in our culture.

2 Movies, music videos, video games, television and the Internet simply reflect the truth about our culture.

3 People who don't like today's media simply should not watch and listen.

4 People learn about life from today's media.

5 Parents should be able to control what their teenagers watch and listen to.

6 I've learned a lot about good and evil, right and wrong from TV, movies, magazines and the Internet.

*Quick Takes Rituals and Retreats* © 1999 by Jean E. Bross, Robert W. Piercy and Dirk deVries. All rights reserved.
Living the Good News, a division of The Morehouse Group. 600 Grant Street, Suite 400, Denver, CO 80203. In U.S. or Canada, call 1-800-824-1813 toll free.

# WORLD PROBLEMS

## JOURNAL #10
### A WARRIOR WITHOUT WEAPONS

Read the story of David and Goliath in 1 Samuel 17:41-51.

In the space below, briefly retell the story in contemporary terms — setting, weapons, enemies, issues at stake, etc. Perhaps it's a senior and a freshman at your school? or an adult and a child in your neighborhood?

Be ready to tell your own version of "David and Goliath" to the group when you regather.

*Quick Takes Rituals and Retreats* © 1999 by Jean E. Bross, Robert W. Piercy and Dirk deVries. All rights reserved.
Living the Good News, a division of The Morehouse Group. 600 Grant Street, Suite 400, Denver, CO 80203. In U.S. or Canada, call 1-800-824-1813 toll free.

# WORLD PROBLEMS

## JOURNAL #11
### POVERTY AND WEALTH

Find Daniel 1:3-16 in your Bible. Read this passage silently.

After you finish reading, consider the following questions, jotting down your answers to questions 5 and 6.

1  Why are Daniel and his friends chosen for the royal court?

2  What problem does this pose for Daniel? (See verse 8.)

3  What deal does Daniel cut with Ashpenaz?

4  What's the result for Daniel and his friends?

5  Daniel made a choice between following God's will and enjoying the pleasures of the king's court...between God and simply indulging himself. When do we face similar choices?

6  What enables us, like Daniel, to choose God?

*Quick Takes Rituals and Retreats* © 1999 by Jean E. Bross, Robert W. Piercy and Dirk deVries. All rights reserved.
Living the Good News, a division of The Morehouse Group. 600 Grant Street, Suite 400, Denver, CO 80203. In U.S. or Canada, call 1-800-824-1813 toll free.

# RELATIONSHIPS

## JOURNAL #13
### TO AN UNKNOWN GOD

Read Acts 17:22-34. Write brief answers for each of the following:

■ How does Paul show respect for the religious beliefs of the Athenians?

■ What is good about the way Paul talks to the people about God? How else might he have handled it?

■ How can we show respect for the religious beliefs of others? What can we learn from Paul about talking to people about our faith?

■ In your opinion, what makes Christianity unique?

Prayer Starter:
Dear God of all peoples, so often my own fear and misunderstanding get in the way of sharing your love with others. Today, help me to reach out in these ways, confident that you are with me...

*Quick Takes Rituals and Retreats* © 1999 by Jean E. Bross, Robert W. Piercy and Dirk deVries. All rights reserved.
Living the Good News, a division of The Morehouse Group. 600 Grant Street, Suite 400, Denver, CO 80203. In U.S. or Canada, call 1-800-824-1813 toll free.

# RELATIONSHIPS

## JOURNAL #14
### LISTEN!

Read Luke 11:5-13. Consider:
- What kind of listener is the friend in Jesus' story? What motivates his "generosity"?
- When has someone "listened" to you in this way, more to get rid of you than because of true caring?

Now read Luke 11:9-10. Consider:
- In contrast to the friend in Jesus' story, these verses describe the way *God* listens. What happens when we ask something of God? seek after God? "knock" at God's door?
- How do we know when God has listened to our asking, seeking and knocking?

Now read Luke 11:11-13. Consider:
- Think of modern versions of Jesus' examples in verses 11-12. For example, "Would any of you give a child paint thinner when they ask for a drink?"
- If human parents listen lovingly to their children, how much more will God! According to Jesus, what kind of listener is God?

Prayer Starter:
Dear Listening God, it means so much to know you care and listen, deeply interested in the details of my life. Listen to me now as I share with you about...

*Quick Takes Rituals and Retreats* © 1999 by Jean E. Bross, Robert W. Piercy and Dirk deVries. All rights reserved.
Living the Good News, a division of The Morehouse Group. 600 Grant Street, Suite 400, Denver, CO 80203. In U.S. or Canada, call 1-800-824-1813 toll free.

# RELATIONSHIPS

## JOURNAL #15
### YES OR NO?

In your Bibles, find and read 1 Samuel 26. Write brief answers for the following questions:

1. Imagine that you are Abishai, trying to convince Dave to kill Saul. What reasons do you give?

2. Imagine that you are God, trying to convince David to spare Saul. What reasons do you give?

3. Imagine that you are David, unsure of the right thing to do. What are you feeling? thinking? What experiences or beliefs do you draw on to make a decision?

4. What difficult moral choices do you and your friends face at school? with friends? with girlfriends or boyfriends? with parents? at work?

5. What gives you direction and strength to do the right thing?

*Quick Takes Rituals and Retreats* © 1999 by Jean E. Bross, Robert W. Piercy and Dirk deVries. All rights reserved.
Living the Good News, a division of The Morehouse Group. 600 Grant Street, Suite 400, Denver, CO 80203. In U.S. or Canada, call 1-800-824-1813 toll free.

# QUICK TAKES RITUALS & RETREATS

# EVALUATION

We want your honest feedback about your experience on this retreat!

Please answer the questions below. Be as specific as possible. General comments like "It was cool!" or "It was awful!" are a good place to start, but telling us *what* was cool (or awful) and *why* it was cool (or awful) will help us better plan future retreats!

Thanks!

The thing I liked best about the retreat was…


The thing I liked least about the retreat was…


If I could change one thing about the retreat, it would be…


One thing that I definitely would like to do on future retreats would be…


On a scale of 1 (poor) to 10 (excellent), I would rate my experience on the retreat as a _____ because…

# THE PRODIGAL STORY

## LUKE 15:11-32 (ADAPTED FROM THE TEV)
### A DRAMATIC READING

**Note:** The story has been adapted to fit female readers as well as male. Use the alternate words, in brackets, as appropriate. If you wish, ad lib.

*Narrator:*
Jesus once told this story: Once a parent had two children. The younger child said to the parent...

*Younger Child:*
Give me my share of the property.

*Narrator:*
So the parent divided the property between the two children.

Not long after that, the younger child packed up everything and left for a foreign country, where he [she] wasted all his [her] money in wild living. The child had spent everything when a bad famine spread through that whole land. Soon he [she] had nothing to eat.

So the child went to work for an employer in that country, who sent him [her] to take care of pigs. The child would have been glad to eat what the pigs were eating, but no one gave him [her] anything.

Finally, he [she] came to his [her] senses...

*Younger child:*
My parent's workers have plenty to eat, and here I am, starving to death! I will go to my parent and say, "I have sinned against God in heaven and against you. I am no longer good enough to be called your child. Treat me like one of your workers."

*Narrator:*
The younger child got up and started back to his [her] parent. But when still a long way of, the parent saw the child and felt sorry for him [her]. The parent ran to the child and hugged and kissed him [her].

The child said...

*Younger Child:*
I have sinned against God and against you. I am no longer good enough to be called your child!

*Narrator:*
But the parent said to the servants...

*Parent:*
Hurry and bring the best clothes and put them on my child. Give him [her] a ring for his [her] finger and sandals for his [her] feet. Get the best calf and prepare it, so we can eat and celebrate. This child of mine was dead, but has now come back to life, was lost and has now been found.

*Narrator:*
And they began to celebrate.

The older child had been out in the field. But when he [she] came near the house, he [she] heard the music and dancing. So he [she] called one of the servants over and asked...

*Older Child:*
What's going on here?

*Narrator:*
The servant answered...

*Servant:*
Your sibling has come home safe and sound, and your parent ordered us to kill the best calf.

*Narrator:*
The older brother [sister] got so angry that he would not even go into the house. The parent came out and begged him [her] to go in. But he [she] said to the parent...

*Older Child:*
For years I have worked for you like a slave and have always obeyed you. But you have never even given me a little goat, so that I could give a dinner for my friends. This other child of yours wasted your money on prostitutes. And now that he [she] has come home, you ordered the best calf to be killed for a feast.

*The Parent:*
My child, you are always with me, and everything I have is yours. But we should be glad and celebrate! Your brother [sister] was dead, but is now alive, was lost and has now been found.

Adapted from the *Today's English Version* Bible. © American Bible Society, 1992. Used by permission.
*Quick Takes Rituals and Retreats* © 1999 by Jean E. Bross, Robert W. Piercy and Dirk deVries. All rights reserved.
Living the Good News, a division of The Morehouse Group. 600 Grant Street, Suite 400, Denver, CO 80203. In U.S. or Canada, call 1-800-824-1813 toll free.

# QUICK TAKES ORDER FORM

## QUICK TAKES FOR TEENS:
### Easy, On-the-Spot Resources for Youth Ministry

Here are the activities you need to create the 12 mini-retreats and 4 weekend retreats included in this book. Each of the 4 *Quick Takes for Teens* volumes gets your teens involved in thinking through important life issues by offering a smorgasbord of creative activities: roleplaying, debates, discussions, games, skits, prayer activities, scripture study, polls and more. Each book focuses on a different area of teen experience: family issues, tough emotions, world problems, and relationship issues.

**4 volumes only $5.95 each**
8 ½" x 5 ½", 48 pages, paperback

To order, complete this form.
**Or for faster service call 1-800-824-1813.**

☐ **Bill to:**
CHURCH _____
ATTN: _____
PHONE (_____) _____
ADDRESS _____
CITY _____
STATE _____ ZIP _____

☐ **Ship to:** (street address required)
CHURCH _____
ATTN: _____
PHONE (_____) _____
ADDRESS _____
CITY _____
STATE _____ ZIP _____

| Quick Takes for Teens | Qty. | Price | Total Amount |
|---|---|---|---|
| Volume 1: Family Issues | | $ 5.95 | |
| Volume 2: Emotions | | $ 5.95 | |
| Volume 3: World Problems | | $ 5.95 | |
| Volume 4: Relationship Issues | | $ 5.95 | |
| SPECIAL OFFER: All 4 volumes | | $ 19.95 | |
| Add sales tax where applicable: PA 6%; CO 3% | | | |
| **Shipping & Handling | | | |
| **Total Due** | | | |

**Shipping and Handling Charges:**
up to $25.00— $4.50
$25.01- $50.00— $5.50
$50.01- $75.00— $7.50
$75.01 and up — $8.50
Outside of U.S., please double rates

## CALL TODAY!
# 1-800-824-1813

*Living the Good News*
a division of The Morehouse Group

**CODE 202**

## ORDERING TIPS:

**By Phone:**
1-800-824-1813

**By Mail:**
Living the Good News, PO Box 1321, Harrisburg, PA 17105

**By Fax:**
717-541-8128

☐ Check enclosed  ☐ Bill my church (**Terms:** Net 30 days)

**We honor these credit cards:** ☐ VISA  ☐ MasterCard

☐☐☐☐☐☐☐☐☐☐☐☐☐☐☐☐
CREDIT CARD NUMBER

☐☐☐ – ☐☐
EXPIRATION DATE

SIGNATURE _____

PRINT NAME _____